Brilliant & Wild

A GARDEN FROM SCRATCH IN A YEAR

Brilliant & Wild

A GARDEN FROM SCRATCH IN A YEAR

LUCY BELLAMY

PHOTOGRAPHS BY JASON INGRAM

PIMPERNEL
PRESS LTD
www.pimpernelpress.com

'People from a planet without flowers would think we must be mad with joy the whole time to have such things about us.'

IRIS MURDOCH

Pimpernel Press Ltd
www.pimpernelpress.com

Brilliant and Wild
Copyright © Pimpernel Press Ltd 2018
Text © Lucy Bellamy 2018
Photographs © Jason Ingram 2018

Design and planting plans by
Becky Clarke

A catalogue record for this book is available from the British Library.

Typeset in ITC Usherwood and Frutiger LT

ISBN 978-1-910258-63-7
Printed and bound in China

9 8 7 6 5 4 3

HALF-TITLE PAGE *Astrantia major* 'Elmblut'
FRONTISPIECE *Anemone* x *hybrida* 'Hadspen Abundance', *Panicum virginatum* 'Shenandoah', *Sanguisorba officinalis* 'Red Buttons'
TITLE PAGE *Allium sphaerocephalon*
RIGHT *Geranium* 'Brookside', *Salvia nemorosa* 'Amethyst', *Rudbeckia occidentalis*, *Stipa tenuissima*

CONTENTS

Eryngium agavifolium, Echinacea pallida and *Verbena bonariensis* grow happily together.

INTRODUCTION

FAT, FLAT-TOPPED SEDUMS IN ROSE AND MULBERRY TONES; QUIVERING GRASSES AND TINY GOSSAMER BLOOMS; UMBRELLA UMBELS ON STOUT STEMS; SHOOTING STARS AND TOWERING SPIRES; JAGGED ERYNGIUMS AND SHARP SPIKES.

In a world of quick-fix, instant-gratification gardening, the brilliant and wild garden is something different. With just a few tools and a back-of-an-envelope plan, it is easy to grow a blooming bee-filled garden from scratch in a single year – a space wild in character that happily knits together in a matter of months, brimming with bugs, birds and butterflies; somewhere that echoes other natural, beautiful places in an incredible sparkling whoosh, wilder, greener and right outside the back door.

In your garden you may have a sad lawn, a rickety fence or an unruly hedge, at one time butchered into submission; or thin borders meanly sliced and spotted with garden-centre singletons in lonely soil. But whether you have a brand new plot or a bedraggled inherited one, the garden before you today won't be the same one you will see in a year's time, even if you do nothing to it at all. All outdoor spaces – including in the wild – are in constant flux. Trying to keep gardens static by means of clipping, cutting and snipping is dull and hard work. Slow-growing plants mean bare soil at first, followed by weeds. Nobody would like gardening if it was all weeding and tidying up.

The garden in a year means a different approach, one with less watering, less weeding, and so less work. It is a thriving community of naturalistic and airy plants, with movement, rhythm and colour pops; a woven matrix of flowers that bloom throughout spring and summer and evolve into a strong and resilient winter silhouette. In the garden in a year you'll find early bloomers and late finishers in a happy tapestry, the transient with the stalwart, the tall supporting the lax, each species matched with appropriate space and company and returning year after year. With no use of insecticides, it will teem with ladybirds and lacewings, honeybees and hoverflies, the beneficial insects enjoying the pollen and nectar while controlling aphids and other pests. It is a garden with a simple annual cycle: each plant is cut back to the soil on the same day, once a year. A meadow of perennials, but on a small scale.

PLANTS ARE THE HEROES
In the brilliant and wild garden, plants are the heroes. This is a thrifty space you can

create by yourself, just digging and planting. The garden uses the wild characteristics of the plants themselves, with clumping, shooting, structural resilience as the backbone to the whole space.

Perennial plants are quick to establish, creating lots of height and flowering within months. Quick to establish is different from fast-growing, which usually means rampant and unruly. One of the joys of using perennials is that a small plant will make a lot of new growth in a single year but without becoming invasive. This means an exhilarating spectacle without spending a lot of money. It's a thrifty way to create a magical space.

The brilliant and wild garden works with the way plants grow, rather than struggling against them. Matching each plant with a

suitable space and using plants that are happy in each other's company means the garden is self-sustaining, and therefore quick and easy to look after in the longer term. Simple combinations are the best ones. Using the natural habits of plants makes this a garden that seemingly grows itself.

The joy of a brilliant and wild garden is that you get almost instant results. It is perfectly possible to plan, prepare and plant it in early spring and be outdoors enjoying it by summer. There's no need to labour and wait.

WILD CHARACTER

The brilliant and wild garden is full of plants with wild character. Choosing simpler, more natural-looking flowers creates an organic garden where the ecosystem thrives. Plants such as these are good news for all sorts of flying insects. Umbels, made of scores of tiny flowerheads, flathead corymbs, composite daisies and tall spires with inbuilt landing platforms on every flower all offer plenty of opportunities for collecting pollen and nectar.

Fussy, elaborate flowers are not attractive to insects. The simpler the flower shape, the easier it is for bees and butterflies to access them. These plants tend to be the ones that look best post-bloom too. Their architectural seedheads echo the shapes of the flowers they once were, and look lovely bleached and backlit in autumn or sunlit in the winter frosts.

BIRDS, BEES AND BUTTERFLIES

The brilliant and wild garden nurtures nature and is alive with ladybirds and lacewings, butterflies and hoverflies, beetles and bees. The whoosh of planting and the repetition of like-with-like plants is easily spotted from on the wing. Clouds of colourful insects, sticky with pollen and drowsy on nectar, make the garden

Anemone × *hybrida* 'Robustissima'

URBAN SPACE

A stylized version of nature with all the best bits, a brilliant and wild garden works well in the urban landscape where small gardens are typically backed by other houses, walls and fences. Juxtaposed with concrete and brick, the wilder planting shines, with a kaleidoscope of differently shaped flowers that look great and hold their shapes even during the winter months.

buzz and hum. Busy insect activity makes a garden (and a planet) thrive. Pollinators zigzag between flowers. Lacewings and ladybirds hunt out sap-sucking aphids, while birds forage for slugs and snails. It's a balanced eco-system where artificial chemical remedies are obsolete. There are nest sites for bumblebees, hibernation spots for ladybirds, bolt holes for mini beasts and nurseries for expectant solitary bees. There is no need for a messy nettle patch or a scruffy, toppling log pile; the brilliant and wild garden is a place where nature reigns.

SEASONAL CHANGE
A brilliant and wild garden is never still. It trumpets a fanfare for every season and celebrates every kind of weather. Shoots shoot, blooms burst, seeds embellish, frost gilds. It is constantly in flux and there is always something new. It's like having a hundred different gardens on a hundred different days.

Slow growing – yawn.

Astrantia 'Roma'

GOODBYE WORK
Hello weekend breakfasts, going out in your socks, having a cup of tea as you watch the clouds. Hello sitting out in the early spring sunshine with a book, or watching the stars at night. Hello sharing a cake on a birthday, an afternoon of sunbathing with a gathering of friends. Hello lunch outside and picking a posy for the kitchen table.

No watering. No room for weeds. Just spring clean with the secateurs once a year.

Yes, please.

From scratch, in a year. 12 months. 365 days.

The newly emerging flower of an echinacea; as the flower matures the ray florets droop gracefully from the central disc.

From scratch in a year

IF YOU ARE LUCKY ENOUGH TO HAVE SOME OUTSIDE SPACE IT'S LOVELY TO FILL IT WITH FLOWERS. EVEN IF YOU ARE NEW TO GROWING THINGS AND LIVE IN THE MIDDLE OF A TOWN OR CITY WITH JUST A SCRATCHY BIT OF SOIL, IT'S POSSIBLE TO MAKE A GARDEN THAT IS QUICK AND EASY TO LOOK AFTER AND READY TO GO IN A MATTER OF MONTHS. ALL YOU NEED IS A SPADE, A FEW GOOD IDEAS AND THE ALCHEMY OF NATURE.

Creating a garden is a fun project. Even if you know very little about soil or how to grow plants, it's simple to create an outdoor space full of shooting stars, fizzing rockets, spikes, globes and ritzy pom-pom flowers that has your own stamp on it and is shaped by your own design.

It's important that a garden is practical as well as pretty, and works day-to-day. You shouldn't have to spend every weekend maintaining it or worry about who will water it when you go on holiday. Choosing flowers that knit together and working with the way plants want to grow is at the heart of a brilliant and wild garden. Every plant in this book works with the others in every combination. You don't need to draw a complicated plan or puzzle over exactly where to put a particular plant. It's all about having a salad bowl of good ideas from which you can pick your favourites; including every plant that you love; letting the garden flourish

and knowing it can take care of itself. It's a beautiful space that's up, off and fully established one year from today.

It's often the case that people feel they will wait until they are living in the perfect house or have reached a particular point in their life before they start a garden. Actually, it's better to start enjoying where you already are. If you never plant anything in case you move on, you will probably find yourself still in the same place a few months later, still wondering if it's worth making a start. Sketching out a plan and choosing your favourite flowers is a Saturday afternoon's work. A few weeks from now you could be outside enjoying your garden.

A garden from scratch in a year doesn't cost a lot of money. In a new perennial garden the plants priovide the structure, so you don't need lots of slabs or bricks or soil; you won't have to hire a digger or pay someone with tools to come and help. After a small initial investment, you don't even need to spend

WHAT IS A PERENNIAL PLANT?

Unlike annuals, which grow, flower, set seed and die within a year, a perennial plant keeps repeating the same cycle every twelve months. Most perennial plants grow in spring from their rootstock underground. They generally flower in summer and often have decorative seedheads that last throughout the coldest months.

much money on plants. Perennial plants in 9cm/3½in pots are not expensive and they're ready to grow quickly. Unlike annuals that have to be pulled out and replaced at the end of every summer, or trees and shrubs that cost a lot of money and may take for ever to reach any meaningful size, perennial plants make a good investment. Smaller plants that cost less get off to a racing start

BETTER FOR THE ENVIRONMENT

When you start to see the activities of visiting bees and ladybirds on your plants or spot your first blackbird searching for lunch, looking after the wider environment begins to feel like the obvious choice. Although your garden is your own space, it's part of the planet that we all share.

Making a garden in a year is a good environmental choice. Because the flowers soar and create the structure you don't need to use a ton of concrete or to ship in big 'instant' plants. Small plants in small pots need less packaging and cost less in fuel miles to transport to garden centres or superstores and then on to you. They don't need weeks of

watering to help them put out roots and settle into unfamiliar soil, so they use less of this valuable resource. Smaller specimens establish quickly and grow into happier, healthier plants that are more able to shrug off pest attacks without resort to chemical sprays. A garden in a year is a garden to plant once and love for ever, so you won't create a constantly growing mountain of unwanted plastic pots.

When nature is thriving on your doorstep it can make a big difference to the way you look at other things too, and you can't help but see you're part of a bigger picture. Making an extra effort with your recycling, using less packaging and thinking twice before buying another plastic bag becomes second nature. It's better for all of us.

BOTANICAL NAMES

Using the botanical names of plants is the only way to know if the plant you are buying online or at a garden centre is definitely the one you intended. Many plants share the same common name, but a botanical name is unique to each plant.

Botanical names usually consist of two or three Latin words. The first, the genus name, is shared by many plants that have similar characteristics. For example, the genus *Echinacea* encompasses all the different echinaceas (coneflowers) in the world, so the name of every coneflower starts with the word *Echinacea,* written in italics. The second word, also italicized, is the species name, which describes a subgroup within the genus, for example *Echinacea pallida*, an echinacea that has pale purple petals (*pallida* translates from Latin as 'pale'). Smaller subgroups may have a third Latinized name in italics, prefaced with 'variety' (var.), subspecies (ssp. or subsp.) or forma (f.).

THE SEASONS

When you're planning a garden, it's vital to know when plants flower. Some bloom non-stop for months on end, while others pop up with the thrill of the new, flower briefly and that's that until the following year. Working out which plants flower at the same time is helpful when you're deciding what you want to include in your garden and how you'll mix and match different plants.

The flowering times for the plants in this book are described as seasons, rather than calendar months, so you can work out when each plant will flower wherever you live.

In the UK the seasons translate as follows:

Mid-winter	January
Late winter	February
Early spring	March
Mid-spring	April
Late spring	May
Early summer	June
Midsummer	July
Late summer	August
Early autumn	September
Mid-autumn	October
Late autumn	November
Early winter	December

A cultivar – that is, a plant that has been selected by a plant-grower as something special and grown to sell – will have an additional name written in Roman type with quotation marks: for example, *Echinacea pallida* 'Hula Dancer'.

The name can tell you a lot about a plant. *Echinacea pallida* 'Hula Dancer' describes a coneflower with a circle of petals that are pale and hang downwards, rippling in the wind, a bit like a dancer's grass skirt.

HAPPY DAYS

Having a garden makes life better. Whether we want somewhere to kick back in the sunshine after work, love having flowers in the house or are simply curious about nature, we all feel better after time outside. Blue skies and fresh air are the perfect counterbalance to our busy days. It's not always possible to pack up the car and head off to the countryside for a weekend's camping or to spread a rug in a field for a picnic lunch, but we can all enjoy a garden on our doorstep.

It's difficult to feel connected to nature and the seasons if we only experience them through the car window. My first garden was in the back of a small terraced house that I lived in for just under a year. It was mostly concrete paving with 3 square metres/32 square feet of soil. I started putting in plants I liked and soon a whole world opened up: a garden that was better than I ever could have imagined, made by nature as much as by me. Since then I've moved many times and everywhere I've lived, I've planted. I always want a space that's full of flowers, bees and butterflies and that can pretty much take care of itself. Making a garden is as much about looking after myself as it is about the plants.

Allium sphaerocephalon and *Knautia macedonica*: brilliant and wild gardens echo wild, magical places.

This wild idea

PLANNING A BRILLIANT AND WILD GARDEN REQUIRES THAT YOU FORGET TRADITIONAL IDEAS ABOUT WHAT A GARDEN IS LIKE. NARROW BORDERS DOTTED WITH PLANTS AT THE EDGES OF A LAWN CONTRIBUTE LITTLE TO THE DAILY PLEASURES OF MODERN LIVING.

Most gardens, even outside brand-new houses, still have their gardens mapped out the traditional way, with a patch of lawn surrounded by borders. The plants are difficult to see from the windows of the house and they can be hard work to care for, too. Many plants will struggle to grow in the strip of shade along the fence created by a typical garden layout. And buying whatever is in flower at the garden centre only to see it fizzle out after a few weeks is dispiriting. When you don't know how a plant grows, how it changes or how quickly, it can be difficut to choose plants that go together and look right. It's easy to end up with a mishmash of plants with gaps between them where weeds take root.

But your garden doesn't have to be like this. A garden can take its cue from the natural landscape. Take a minute to imagine a beautiful, wild space, with a narrow path through a flower-filled meadow – a magical place growing according to nature's rules but in your town or city space.

Salvia nemorosa 'Caradonna': using flowers close to the house allows you to see them every time you pop outside.

It's not always necessary to buy new tools. You might be able to borrow or buy tools that have been used and loved.

TOOLS

This is a garden for which you need only a few basic tools. It's not always necessary to buy new equipment – you might be able to borrow a spade for an afternoon's planting, or pick up a second-hand one at little cost. Charity shops often have garden tools that have already been used and loved but are no longer needed. Look for handles that feel solid and sturdy and check that there isn't any rust.

SPADE You will find spades on sale in different shapes, sizes and weights. The tip of the spade is a blade used to cut down into the soil, slicing out lumps of earth for lifting. The handle needs to be strong enough to hold the weight of the soil without bending or buckling but still feel comfortable in your hands.

WATERING CAN This can be as big as you can lift once it is heavy and full of water – a larger can saves multiple trips to the tap. Every new young plant will need thorough soaking with water when it is first in the ground to settle the soil around its roots and encourage new ones to grow. After this the rain will do the hard work for you.

SECATEURS You'll need secateurs for the once-a-year spring cut back. It's probably worth buying new secateurs as they must be sharp, so that they cut rather than crush stems.

HAND TROWEL Planting bulbs and digging out stubborn weeds before starting the planting is easier with a small trowel, though you can use your spade for these jobs too.

DESIGN

The medley of plants that make up a brilliant and wild garden will itself create the structure of the garden. Wilder planting needs a strong design. Where you place your plants is key to making it a brilliant space. Plan one big area, at least 1m/3¼ft deep, to fill with plants, crossing the garden horizontally. In a small garden this might take up almost the whole of your outside space, with just a little left for chairs and a table next to the back door. In a bigger garden you might plan two separate areas for your plants, with some grass left between them. Wide geometric borders give a contemporary look. Straight edges and square corners make a space look bold and purposeful and create the perfect foil for the jostle of plants to come.

Putting the plants close to the house and across the garden rather than just at the sides means you will see your flowers every time you go outside, even if you're only popping out to take a bag to the bin or to check the weather.

Echinacea pallida, Eryngium agavifolium, Perovskia 'Blue Spire'

Soil is made up of sand silt and clay plus organic matter such as rotting plant material.

Plants need to be carefully firmed in.

YOUR SOIL

The soil is an ecosystem, and it's important for it to be healthy and thriving. Soil is made up of sand, silt and clay in differing amounts, plus organic matter such as rotting leaves. Soils can be very thin or stony, in which case they struggle to keep hold of any moisture. If you have a new house or building work has taken place nearby there may even be rubble in the soil. At the opposite end of the scale soils may be heavy, compacted and full of water in winter but baked hard and dry in summer. Urban soils are often exhausted, dusty and low in nutrients.

Poor urban soils are perfect for a garden in a year. Their lower fertility creates plants that are tough and strong and won't collapse in heavy winds or turn into a soggy mush as soon as the cold weather hits. No one species races away and takes over. The plants grow in tandem and establish themselves according to their own rules, just as they would in nature. Bright blue perovskia spires, whorled purple salvias, pom-pom alliums, eryngiums with thistle-flowers, and the bobbled orange daisies of heleniums; skinnier soils support plants such as these.

NEW PERSPECTIVES

Plants are the heart and soul of a garden made in a year, standing front and centre. They are the stars of the show. Soaring verbenas spangled with purple flowers, long-stemmed echinaceas and grasses shimmering like mist; the brilliant and wild garden includes plants to look through and over. Traditional borders with a fence or wall behind them only get the sunlight from the front, which makes their aspect – whether they face north, south, east or west – much more important. On the north side of the fence, a flower that loves sunshine will never be at its best.

Tall, airy planting stretched across the garden lets the sunlight shine through. Many flowers look lovely backlit by the sun. Petals glow like stained glass and a burst of slanting sunshine on an otherwise grey day will turn grasses golden. As the sun moves across the sky, patterns of light and shade are created. Everything is open to the light and air.

Nepeta racemosa 'Walker's Low' and *Salvia* × *sylvestris* 'Viola Klose'

HOW TO DIG

The roots of plants need water and oxygen as well as minerals from the soil, so the purpose of digging is to break up the earth, adding pockets of air and helping water to pass through. You'll only need to dig your garden once. You can do it at any time of year, though it's best to avoid very wet or cold days as you risk squashing wet soil back down as quickly as you dig it up.

- Dig in rows, moving from left to right and working backwards so that you're standing on the soil you'll dig next.
- Use the tip of your spade like a blade to cut straight down, making a cube of soil that's the same width.
- Push the spade underneath the cube, lift it and turn it over.

After you've finished, the soil will be slightly raised because of the air you've added. Ideally, dig your soil a week or two before you want to start planting, otherwise level the top and it will settle back down over time.

Making a start

TODAY IS THE BEST DAY TO START YOUR NEW
GARDEN. SPRING, SUMMER, AUTUMN OR WINTER,
START ON ANY DAY.

Your brilliant and wild garden is waiting to grow, and ready to begin the same day you are. Using small pot-grown plants means you can start planting at any time of year as long as the ground isn't frozen.

Because the plants form the structure of the garden, it's important to think about where everything will go. It's best to plan your garden outside. Even with careful measuring, sitting at the kitchen table is no substitute for being out in the garden at the planning stage and taking a good look at the space you have.

Start by thinking about the best position for the main planting area. Your planting is for looking into, across and through. It's usually best to have your main border close to the door, or where you sit when you go outside.

Push sticks into the ground to act as markers for where you want the patches of plants to start and finish. Tying a piece of twine between the sticks and pulling it taut creates a straight line that makes it easier to see how things will look. Try putting the sticks and string in a few different places, moving them forwards and backwards to change the size and shape of the planting area.

Once you've settled on a planting area, it's useful to go back into the house and look at it through the windows. This perspective will quickly tell you if the area you've allocated needs to be wider, bigger or in a slightly different spot. In a small space, it's fine to leave a patch of lawn that's only the width of a path.

When you're happy with everything, use the tip of the spade to cut vertically down alongside the string and mark a neat edge. If there is grass inside the area, cut small squares in it with the tip of your spade and then slide the spade beneath them to lift them away. Soil that has been under a patch of grass is likely to be quite compacted where people have been walking on it, so you will need to dig it over. You don't need to dig very deeply – just far enough down break up any compaction. Remove any perennial weeds such as dandelions and couch grass.

kit

TWINE OR STRING
STICKS, TO USE AS
MARKERS
SPADE
TAPE MEASURE

Use sticks and twine to plan your garden's layout. It's easy to move them about and try out different ideas.

Tie the twine to the sticks using a bow so that you can easily make adjustments to the placing of them should you want to.

Straight lines make everything look bold and purposeful, and are the perfect foil for the whoosh of the flowers to come. Pulling the twine taut creates a perfect straight line.

Use a spade to cut an edge and remove any unwanted grass.

Dig over the new planting space, especially in spots that have become solid and compacted.

Teucrium hircanicum
and *Stachys officinalis*
'Hummelo'

The plants

CHOOSING THE RIGHT PLANTS IS KEY. CREATING A BRILLIANT AND WILD GARDEN IS A BIT LIKE ARRANGING A BUNCH OF FLOWERS, PICKING DIFFERENT SHAPES, MAKING PATTERNS AND THINKING ABOUT HOW EVERYTHING GOES (AND GROWS) TOGETHER.

You don't need to be an experienced gardener to make a beautiful garden, but if you just buy whatever looks pretty at the garden centre on a particular day you can end up with a bit of a mishmash. Without a little research in advance, you won't know how things change and grow.

SHAPE

Some flowers spend all summer growing as tall as they can in a race for the skies. Others produce thousands of miniature flowers, spreading them out flat, like tiny dinner plates, so plenty of pollinators are tempted to visit. The fat centres of daisies are round like doorknobs, surrounded by a ray of petals, one neat ball atop every stalk. There are thistle flowers, starry umbels and grasses with seeds like grains of rice. The mixture of heights, shapes and textures is the alchemy that will make your garden dazzle. Different shapes will create changes of pace and energy, pockets of excitement and quieter spots; they are also the best way to make a space that straddles the seasons

Astrantia major 'Large White'

without you having to add extra plants later on, as their seedheads echo the shapes of their flowers and decorate the garden in the colder months.

It's best to choose just two or three flower shapes and use plenty of different species that share that shape – for example, umbels with spikes, or panicles with flatheads and dots. Repeating the same shapes creates rhythm. Even if your flowers were planted completely at random, there would still be harmony and balance.

PATTERN

The patterns in nature are hard to beat; pick and mix meadows, woven tapestries and tessellating patchworks of repeating plants. Even the simplest wild scene is usually a combination of several different plants.

Repeating the same plants, and setting them together in groups, is an easy way to create a brilliant garden. Two or three plants of the same species growing together look bold and confident. Every plant looks better in the company of its peers; seen close up the individual flowers are easier to appreciate, and big blocks of colour look fantastic from further away.

Repeating groups of the same plant throughout the space will link your garden together. Showstoppers and champion bloomers intermingling with clumps of less showy species create lovely notes of contrast. Putting different flowers together and creating pretty juxtapositions is fun. You can use different-sized groups with different numbers of plants and repeat the groups different numbers of times too.

TOP RIGHT *Allium hollandicum*
BOTTOM RIGHT *Verbena bonariensis*

ECOLOGY

In a happy community of flowers everything is growing together, doing its thing and finding its own space. Planting like-with-like – flowers that grow in the same way and benefit from the same conditions – is the best way to a self-sustaining space and a constantly changing palette where there is always something new to see.

Plants that go together and grow together can be treated as a whole, rather than as individuals. They make a space that is simple to look after but where there's still lots to see. No plant needs special treatment. Letting everything knit together as it grows means that each plant will find its own favourite spot. Ecologists describe the way plants arrange themselves as following 'assembly rules'.

KEEP IT SIMPLE

The trickiest part of creating a garden from scratch is keeping it simple. Big, firework actaeas, sparkler alliums, velvety anenomes and gorgeous, blingy dahlias; once you start delving into the wonderful world of flowers it's very easy to find plenty of lovely blooms that make your heart skip a beat. You'll want to include them all. However, while it's tempting to put in every flower you like, gardens are always much better when the palette of plants used is limited in some way.

Shape, pattern and ecology are at the heart of this, but there are other factors that can help you to refine your choices too.

HEIGHT

As you start to compile a list of favourite flowers, it's useful to write down the different heights they will grow to and group them into tall, medium and shorter plants. Tall plants are anything that grows over 1.2m/4ft;

Allium hollandicum, Astrantia major 'Claret' and *Nepeta* 'Walker's Low'

medium plants grow to 0.6–1.2m/2–4ft; and short plants are those that reach less than 0.6m/2ft when they are fully grown. Plants in each height range have different roles to play in your garden, and they work together in different ways.

Shorter plants are perfect for creating a framework for other plants to grow through. Florists often refer to 'filler' flowers in a bouquet, and shorter plants are the equivalent outside. Use them as a starting point, choosing a mixture of one or two flower shapes to create a matrix that the taller plants will grow through. Using some medium-height plants as part of this will add undulations and new textures, and stop this lower storey looking too flat.

Echinacea pallida

It's hard to overestimate the importance of height in any garden, especially a new one. Taller plants include plumes, spires and hazy clouds of panicles as well as bolder shapes like dots. Those that grow tall quickly but don't take over have a vital role to play in a small space. The stems of plants such as these tend to be leafless, as the plants use all of their energy to gain extra height. The skinny stems show off the shapes of their flowers brilliantly, plus they don't shade out shorter plants underneath. They can get all of the sunlight they need to grow too.

Tall plants can also be useful planted individually, scattered here and there or planted in ribbons to tie a garden together. Plants such as alliums and *Rudbeckia occidentalis* are fantastic for this. Planting just a few and giving them some space above the other flowers means you can really appreciate their shapes.

FLOWERING TIME

Choosing flowers that start and finish at different times, and flower for different lengths of time, makes a garden that looks a treat for longer and always has the promise of more good things to come. Mix early flowerers and late finishers, choose flowers that are at their best at different times of year and plan some overlaps too. In this way the garden will mirror the changing seasons and connect the garden to what is happening outside. Even a tiny space can have more than 300 days of new blooms.

COLOUR

Colourful petals are only one part of what makes a garden great, but they can be an important part. You wouldn't want to fill your house with a clashing jamboree of mismatched hues and the same is true of the garden. Theming your plant choice around a favourite colour can stop it looking too busy.

Think sky blue, deep blue and iridescent purple or pale lemon and sunshine yellow with brilliant orange shots.

Plants with wild character tend to have more green parts (leaves and stems) than modern hybrids, which have often been bred to create the biggest and most blowsy flowers possible. Using wilder plants makes it much easier to create colour combinations that won't jar.

AGM PLANTS

Some plants have the letters AGM or 🏆 after their name. You'll see it when you look on the plant label or search for a plant online. It indicates that the plant has gained an 'Award of Garden Merit', which means that it has been tried and tested by the RHS (Royal Horticultural Society) and has been noted as one of the best of its type. Plants that are awarded the AGM are 'excellent for garden use', so this is a good guideline when you are struggling to choose between two similar plants, just one of which has an AGM.

Using flowers from different groups is an easy way to make sure you include a mixture of umbels, spikes, dots and panicles. It will also guarantee your garden looks incredible even in the colder, trickier months.

Each plant in this book will work with the others in any combination and you'll be able to obtain all of them easily. Most are available online and from nurseries all year round, and you'll find them in garden centres too during the months they are in flower.

The pincushion flowers and white bracts of *Astrantia major* last for weeks in the garden.

Umbellifers

AN UMBEL IS AN INFLORESCENCE THAT HAS THE SHAPE OF AN OPEN UMBRELLA, WITH SMALL, STAR-LIKE BLOOMS RADIATING OUT FROM THE TOP OF THE STEM.

With constellations of starry flowers atop straight stems, umbellifers will reconnect your garden with beautiful, wild places. The umbel is the predominant flower shape in the natural landscape. With clean lines and simple symmetry that make clear, crisply shaped plants, umbellifers have an airy grace.

Plant one umbellifer with another and they will intermingle, creating a loose matrix of stems and gentle curves of flowers. While they will echo each other in shape they can be used to create contrasts, particularly if they are different sizes or heights. Umbellifers also work well with skyward-reaching spikes: the juxtaposition of the shapes, one across, one up, creates a change of rhythm that will energize a small space.

Repeating groups of umbels are great for connecting different sections of planting. They add height, but because of their airiness you can still see through to the flowers behind. They make happy company for other tall flowers – for example, a stiff eryngium stalk will keep a thalictrum upright, avoiding the need for stakes and twine.

Umbellifers are all in the family Apiaceae and they grow from tap roots – a long, chunky root that looks like a carrot or a parsnip and grows straight down into the soil, rather than spreading out sideways. The flowers and leaves all grow from one central point at the top of the root and they don't send out runners that pop up in unexpected places in the garden and need digging out.

Because their stems are mostly leafless, umbellifers combine easily with other flowers; the foliage is mainly around the base of the plants, so they don't block the light or the rain from other plants close by.

The name Apiaceae is derived from *apium*, the Latin word for wild celery, which in turn came from *apis*, meaning bee. All Apiaceae flowers have lots of pollen and nectar; they hum with bees. You can also expect hoverflies, lacewings, butterflies, moths and tiny predatory wasps (which eat aphids) to visit the flowers.

Particularly in a small garden, it's important that the plants can straddle the seasons. Most umbellifers start into growth early, soaring in spring and bursting into flower by the beginning of summer. Although they look delicate, the flowers are typically very long-lasting, and in autumn the seedheads echo the umbrella shapes of the original flowers. They'll last into winter as skeletons glittering in frost.

ANTHRISCUS

Anthriscus sylvestris 'Ravenswing' is a dark-foliaged version of the cow parsley that grows at the sides of country roads – a flower that says road trips, picnics and long country walks. It has lacy leaves with a plummy hue and just like its wild cousin it's topped with white doilies of small flowers on jauntily angled stems.

Anthriscus starts growing early in the year and is tall and flowering by late spring, when most plants are just leafing up. The flowers are popular with hoverflies, bees and small beetles, which pollinate them as they go. In summer they are replaced by black oval seeds at the tips of the stalks.

This is a shorter-lived perennial, so it makes itself more reliable by gently resowing its patch. If you are lucky enough to have

anthriscus set seed in your garden, in spring look for the seedlings with black leaves. These are the ones to keep, as they'll grow up to have the same dark stems and white flowers

Anthriscus sylvestris 'Ravenswing'

BOTANICAL NAME *Anthriscus sylvestris* 'Ravenswing'

COMMON NAME Queen Anne's lace

FAMILY Apiaceae

WHY GROW IT?
White flowers from late spring to midsummer; deep purple foliage.

WILDLIFE BENEFITS
Pollen and nectar source for bees and hoverflies; winter homes in the hollow stems for hibernating solitary bees, ladybirds, hoverflies, lacewings and their larvae.

SIZE Height 1.2m/4ft; spacing 5 per square metre/11 square feet.

as the original plants. However, *Anthriscus sylvestris* 'Ravenswing' won't seed about so much that it becomes a nuisance.

GOES WELL WITH . . .

FLOWERS *Nectaroscordum siculum* (Sicilian honey garlic), *Astrantia* 'Hadspen Blood' (masterwort), *Dianthus carthusianorum* (German pink)

GRASSES *Stipa tenuissima* (feather grass)

Astrantia major 'Claret'

ASTRANTIA

BOTANICAL NAME *Astrantia*

COMMON NAME Hattie's pincushion, masterwort

FAMILY Apiaceae

WHY GROW IT?
Jewel colours; flowers from late spring to late summer; long-lasting seedheads.

BEST CULTIVARS
A. 'Hadspen Blood', *A. major* 'Claret', *A. major* 'Elmblut', *A. major* 'Large White', *A.* 'Roma'

WILDLIFE BENEFITS
Four months of pollen and nectar for bees, hoverflies and butterflies; winter homes for ladybirds.

SIZE Height 60cm/24in; spacing 5 per square metre/11 square feet.

The umbels of astrantia are quite small – you have to be sharp-eyed to spot that its round, pincushion blooms are made up of multiple tiny flowers, crowded inside a ruff of papery bracts. People often mistake the bracts for petals as they are wonderfully coloured and often beautifully marked, luminous when the sun shines through.

'Astra' translates from Latin as 'star' and every astrantia is like a meteor shower. It is a magical flower to grow, with clusters of blooms on pin-thin stems that look like miniature galaxies. Using it with flowers of different shapes is key.

Astrantia flowers in ruby red, pink and pearly white. *A. major* 'Claret' is the richest red, with nearly black stems and plum-tinged leaves that look as if they have been dipped in ink. 'Roma' is pink and dusky with bright green leaves that capture the freshness of spring. *A. major* 'Large White' is bigger, with apple green bracts tipped in pale pink.

Pink and white astrantias work well in a fresh, bright scheme. They are also the best flowers to choose for shady spots as they shine out on gloomier days. I like 'Large White' with the big green umbellifer *Mathiasella* and *Stipa tenuissima*, the feather grass. Even under an overcast sky it's a combination that looks bright.

Insects love astrantia; bumblebees, solitary bees, beetles and hoverflies will all visit the flowers. It's one of the longest-blooming perennial plants, with flowers that start in late spring and continue apace into autumn, each one lasting for several weeks. If you want to you can snip off the first fading flowers to encourage extra to develop, or you can just leave it to do its own thing.

Astrantia works hard to straddle the seasons. When the weather turns colder the flowers fade and turn papery, but they still keep their shape. The seedheads are small but robust and they will withstand the coldest weather, decorating your garden throughout the winter months and into the start of spring.

GOES WELL WITH . . .

FLOWERS *Nectaroscordum siculum* (Sicilian honey garlic), *Anthriscus sylvestris* 'Ravenswing' (black cow parsley), *Allium hollandicum* 'Purple Sensation' (ornamental onion)

GRASSES *Stipa tenuissima* (feather grass)

ERYNGIUM

Eryngium agavifolium has thimble flowers atop tall stems.

BOTANICAL NAME *Eryngium*
COMMON NAME Sea holly
FAMILY Apiaceae
WHY GROW IT?
Tall architectural shape; physical support for companions; striking shades of blue, purple or reddish-brown flowers from early summer to late summer.
BEST SPECIES
E. agavifolium, E. eburneum, E. ebracteatum var. *poterioides, E.* × *tripartitum* (AGM), *E. yuccifolium*
WILDLIFE BENEFITS
Pollen and nectar source for bees and hoverflies, nectar source for butterflies. Winter homes in the hollow stems for hibernating bees, ladybirds, hoverflies, lacewings and their larvae.
SIZE Height 1.2m/4ft; spacing 3 per square metre/11 square feet.

As you might expect from the common name of sea holly, eryngiums are decidedly spiky. The flowers are shaped like thimbles, narrow and tight, and held inside barbed bracts, while the leaves are jagged, with sharp teeth.

In spring, eryngiums produce a rosette of leaves. The flower stalks grow from the middle of this and are topped with bobbled flowers. The plants can be silver-green, blue or purplish, some even rather metallic in effect, and in a very sunny spot a blue eryngium will become even stronger in colour.

GOES WELL WITH . . .

FLOWERS *Echinacea pallida* (pale coneflower), *Helenium* 'Moerheim Beauty' (autumn daisy), *Rudbeckia occidentalis* (western coneflower)
GRASSES *Deschampsia cespitosa* 'Goldtau' (tufted hair grass), *Panicum virgatum* 'Shenandoah' (switch grass)

Eryngiums knit together easily with other tall flowers. I like them jostling for space with other dots like echinacea and helenium or perovskia spikes. Bees and hoverflies love the pollen-packed flowers and it's not unusual to see more than one type of pollinator vying for space on one plant.

Eryngium ebracteatum, the Paraguay sword plant, is a different sort of sea holly. It has wiry stems that are like a candelabra, very tight red umbels and swords for leaves. It flowers a bit earlier than other eryngiums and is best given some space to shine.

After their summer display, eryngiums produce beautiful winter seedheads that will make your garden work as a four-season space.

FOENICULUM

BOTANICAL NAME *Foeniculum vulgare*

COMMON NAME Fennel

FAMILY Apiaceae

WHY GROW IT?
Catherine-wheel flowers from midsummer to late summer; feathery foliage; pretty seedheads.

BEST CULTIVAR
F. vulgare 'Purpureum'

WILDLIFE BENEFITS
Pollen and nectar for smaller pollinating insects including solitary bees, hoverflies, soldier beetles, damsel bugs, flower bugs, shield bugs and mini braconid wasps – beneficial insects that are predators of caterpillars and aphids. Winter homes in the hollow stems for hibernating bees, ladybirds, hoverflies, lacewings and their larvae.

SIZE Height 2m/7ft; spacing 4 per square metre/11 square feet.

Foeniculum vulgare

Fennel flowerheads explode like Catherine wheels, with thousands of tiny yellow blooms that grow from bright green buds. The umbels are so perfectly formed that they look as if they have been drawn with a pencil and a ruler; taut stems, perfect symmetry and a curve of lacy flowers.

Fennel is a great way to bring a bit of wildness into your garden. Green-leaved varieties can seed about quite a lot and become a bit of a nuisance, but the bronze varieties sow themselves more gently. The shape of their leaves makes the seedlings easy to identify and pull out if you want to.

Fennel flowers last a long time and in autumn the chunky seeds appear to replace them; they look almost too big for the stalks but are a very pretty sight. When they darken and fall off they leave behind a claw of bracts amid a mass of feathery foliage that stays throughout winter and makes it a great four-season plant.

The flowers are visited frequently by foraging insects, especially smaller ones such as solitary bees, damsel bugs, shield bugs and soldier beetles. The small flowers are perfect for their tiny mouthparts. The seeds are a good food source for birds plumping up ready for winter as they are rich in oils and energy.

GOES WELL WITH . . .

FLOWERS *Anemone × hybrida* 'Königin Charlotte' (windflower), *Actaea simplex* 'James Compton' (bugbane)

GRASSES *Deschampsia cespitosa* 'Goldtau' (tufted hair grass)

MATHIASELLA

Mathiasella bupleuroides 'Green Dream'; the green flowers are edged with red, echoing the colour of the stems.

BOTANICAL NAME *Mathiasella bupleuroides*

COMMON NAME Mathiasella

FAMILY Apiaceae

WHY GROW IT?
Large umbels of green flowers from late spring to midsummer; architectural seedheads.

BEST CULTIVAR
M. bupleuroides 'Green Dream'

WILDLIFE BENEFITS
Large flowers that are a pollen and nectar source for bumblebees; winter homes in the hollow stems for hibernating bees, ladybirds, hoverflies, lacewings and their larvae.

SIZE Height 1m/3¼ft; spacing 1–3 per square metre/11 square feet.

When we consider the role of green in the landscape or garden we are most likely to think of leaves, stems and grasses, but of course flowers can be green too. Some green flowers look anything but natural. Those found in supermarket bouquets have often been coloured with dye in lurid shades or bred from flowers that aren't inherently green. Naturally green flowers are very different from these: fresh and bright and full of life, they remind us of wild places where nature comes and goes as it likes. Most people love green flowers as soon as they see them and want to know how they can grow some themselves. They look unusual, but in a good way.

Mathiesella is an architectural plant with bright apple-green flowers that are held in a distinctive umbel shape, and last for months. They mix easily with other flowers and are particularly good with astrantias – which are also umbels but smaller – or with bright, loose grasses that throw the umbel shape into contrast.

Mathasiella is a popular plant with bumblebees, as the florets that make up its umbel are big enough for a fat bee to crawl right into. As with all umbellifers, its strong, hollow stem lasts throughout winter, making a good spot for ladybirds and lacewings to hibernate.

GOES WELL WITH . . .

FLOWERS *Astrantia major* 'Claret' (Hattie's pincushion), *Cirsium rivulare* 'Atropurpureum' (plume thistle)

GRASSES *Stipa tenuissima* (feather grass), *Deschampsia cespitosa* 'Goldtau' (tufted hair grass)

PIMPINELLA

BOTANICAL NAME *Pimpinella major*

COMMON NAME Pimpinella

FAMILY Apiaceae

WHY GROW IT?

Loose, airy umbels; looks like a wild flower; blooms from late spring to midsummer.

BEST CULTIVAR

P. major 'Rosea'

WILDLIFE BENEFITS

Pollen and nectar source for bees and hoverflies, nectar for butterflies; winter homes in the hollow stems for hibernating bees, ladybirds, hoverflies, lacewings and their larvae.

SIZE Height 60cm/24in; spacing 5 per square metre/11 square feet.

Loose and airy pimpinella has umbels like a pink cow parsley held atop stiff stems. It knits together easily with other umbellifers, creating a loose matrix of stalks and flowers. The pretty flowerheads, with lots of flowers full of pollen and nectar clustered together, are mecca for insects. Pimpinella is particularly popular with smaller pollinators.

Pimpinella grows on tap roots and new flower stalks grow from around the base. It gains height more quickly than it spreads and adds plenty of height to a small space. It can seed about where there is any bare soil, which will add to the spontaneity of your garden, enhancing a wild effect.

Pimpinella major 'Rosea' has a loose umbel shape that knits together easily with other plants.

GOES WELL WITH . . .

FLOWERS *Perovskia* 'Blue Spire' (Russian sage), *Verbena macdougalii* 'Lavender Spires'

GRASSES *Stipa tenuissima* (feather grass)

Spikes

WITH A STRONG VERTICAL LINE AND SMALL FLOWERS ON STRAIGHT STEMS, SPIKES REACH FOR THE SKIES.

A spike is a plant with points of flowers that grow straight up. With their strong imperative to grow vertically, tall spikes are good for adding height fast – very important in a new garden. An inky salvia or an actaea with its white bottlebrush flowers silhouetted against the sky is a lovely thing.

Plant spikes closely together to make layers of colour. Smaller spikes look best in groups of three or more, but just one or two of the bigger plants will work well. Spikes provide crowds of colourful flowers that other plants can grow through and are brilliant with dots for a contrast of shape, while grasses echo their verticals.

Flowers borne on a spike are good for pollinators that like to hover, as well as for those that prefer to land as they forage. The tiny trumpet flowers of a nepeta attract bumblebees, honeybees and small solitary bees. Like most spikes, nepetas open over consecutive days from the bottom to the top, so that some flowers will be open and full of nectar while others are still in bud. Pollinators can revisit the flowers on consecutive days.

With an urge to go up and stay up, most spikes have very robust stalks, so they make the best winter seedheads. In cold weather a phlomis turns charcoal black while perovskia is ghostly white, providing long-lasting interest in what can be a sparse time of year in the garden.

LEFT *Salvia × sylvestris* 'Viola Klose'
RIGHT *Nepeta racemosa* 'Walker's Low'
with *Salvia nemorosa* 'Cardamine'

ACTAEA

Actaea simplex 'James Compton'

BOTANICAL NAME *Actaea simplex*
COMMON NAME Bugbane
FAMILY Ranunculaceae
WHY GROW IT?
  Tall bottlebrush flowers; flowers from early to late autumn; winter seedheads.
BEST CULTIVAR
  A. simplex 'James Compton' AGM
WILDLIFE BENEFITS
  Pollen and nectar source for hoverflies and bees, nectar for butterflies.
SIZE Height 1.5m/5ft; spacing 4 per square metre/11 square feet.

Actaea is a very tall spike with white bottlebrush flowers held at the tops of long bronze stems. It flowers in autumn and high up, so the flowers catch the last of the sunlight. Its large leaves are also bronze. They appear in early summer and for a while it's a sultry foliage plant. When it soars it has strong stems and, like most spikes, can be a good support for more lax plants. Actaea works well with airy grasses such as deschampsia. Its flowers are great weaving amid deschampsia's haze.

When the weather turns colder, actaea makes striking black silhouettes that stand against the sky and last all winter.

GOES WELL WITH . . .

FLOWERS *Anemone hupehensis* 'Hadspen Abundance' (windflower), asters, *Foeniculum vulgare* 'Purpureum' (bronze fennel), **GRASSES** *Deschampsia cespitosa* 'Goldtau' (tufted hair grass)

AGASTACHE

BOTANICAL NAME *Agastache*

COMMON NAME Giant hyssop

FAMILY Lamiaceae

WHY GROW IT?
Long flowering season; violet-blue flowers from midsummer to early autumn; arrow seedheads.

BEST CULTIVAR
A. 'Blackadder' AGM

WILDLIFE BENEFITS
Densely flowered, with pollen and nectar for bees, nectar for butterflies.

SIZE Height 90cm/36in spacing 6 per square metre/11 square feet.

Agastache 'Blackadder'

The purple, blue and violet bottlebrush flowers of agastache are held on spikes that point straight to the sky. The leaves are below them, on the lower half of the stems. They smell of liquorice and lemon when you crush them with your fingers.

Agastache works well planted cheek by jowl with salvia and perovskia as repeating spikes. The three plants knit together easily where they meet but don't try to take over each other's space, instead making layers of different colours.

Planting agastache with grasses brings out its prairie nature. Swirling *Stipa tenuissima* matches its stiffness with smudginess. The grass grows to the same height as the agastache and adds movement to the mix.

Agastache spikes have lots of small flowers, densely packed together. The flowers are violet-blue, easily spotted from the wing, and the plentiful supplies of pollen and nectar make it a good choice for bees.

The flowers evolve into seedheads that become darker the colder it gets. They'll stand like a quiver of arrows and decorate your garden in winter, glinting and shimmering, rimed with frost.

GOES WELL WITH . . .

FLOWERS *Perovskia* 'Blue Spire' (Russian sage), *Salvia nemorosa* 'Caradonna' (meadow sage), *Echinacea* (coneflower)

GRASSES *Stipa tenuissima* (feather grass)

NEPETA

Nepeta racemosa 'Walker's Low' and Rudbeckia occidentalis

BOTANICAL NAME *Nepeta racemosa*
COMMON NAME Catmint
FAMILY Lamiaceae
WHY GROW IT?
   Tiny trumpet flowers borne from early summer to early autumn, even during a bad summer; pretty chalky leaves.
BEST CULTIVAR
   N. racemosa 'Walker's Low'
WILDLIFE BENEFITS
   Densely packed flowers with pollen and nectar for bees and hoverflies, nectar for butterflies; soft, downy leaves for the wool carder bee to use for nest-building.
SIZE Height 60cm/24in; spacing 3 per square metre/11 square feet.

Crush the leaves of *Nepeta racemosa* and they smell of lemons and spice; aromatic and musky, reminiscent of hot nights in far-flung places. The tiny trumpet flowers are the brightest blue and almost iridescent. Together they create a soft blue-washed haze above the pale, chalky foliage, like a pointillist painting.

Nepeta is quite a lax spike, with a slight tendency to loll. It will happily survive the odd flipflop or wellington boot at the edge of the lawn, releasing its fragrance when you stand on it, and it adds a lovely looseness to other plants. Because the stems grow from a central point it doesn't spread wildly about, but its lushness and lounging habit means it thoroughly covers the soil nearby, limiting opportunities for weeds.

The soft washed blues and green leaves of summer are fantastic with other chalky colours; buttery achillea, pink and purple salvia and violet-blue perovskia. Nepeta is very long-flowering and it overlaps both early and late summer plants.

All sorts of flying insects love the small flowers and they are always smothered in bees. Every trumpet flower has a protruding lip, or landing pad, that makes it an easy plant for pollinators to visit. The flowers are crowded together, perfect for busy workers, and packed with nectar. They are perfect for carder and small garden bees that have long tongues to reach inside. Short-tongued bees such as buff-tailed and white-tailed bumblebees bite small holes into the base of the flowers, just above the stalk, and get at the nectar that way.

Nepeta leaves are covered in tiny, fine hairs which make it a good plant for a sunny spot. It doesn't wilt during very hot weather, even if water is scarce and other plants start to flag.

Nepeta racemosa 'Walker's Low'. Planting some nepeta will make your garden hum with bees in early summer.

GOES WELL WITH . . .
FLOWERS *Salvia nemorosa* 'Caradonna' (meadow sage), *Achillea* 'Terracotta' (yarrow), *Perovskia* 'Blue Spire' (Russian sage)
GRASSES *Sesleria autumnalis* (autumn moor grass)

PEROVSKIA

Perovskia 'Blue Spire'

BOTANICAL NAME *Perovskia*
COMMON NAME Russian sage
FAMILY Lamiaceae
WHY GROW IT?
Strong vertical shape; flowers from midsummer to early autumn; white stems in winter.
BEST CULTIVAR
P. 'Blue Spire'
WILDLIFE BENEFITS
Pollen and nectar source for bees, nectar source for butterflies.
SIZE Height 1m/3¼ft; spacing 4 per square metre/11 square feet.

Perovskia's purple velvet buds and tiny trumpet flowers create a blue haze in the second half of summer. The flowers are dotted up and down the stems and spaced widely apart so the plant looks light and bright. Because its narrow, pale stems are sturdy but not rigidly so, it's a good companion to more lax plants.

Perovskia pairs well with chunky sedum flatheads which emphasize its strongly upward habit, or with echinacea or anemone heads on tall skinny stems. In winter, after the flowers fade, its stems create a ghostly outline that shines out on gloomy days and looks good with darker seedheads. It likes a sunny spot.

It's a member of the sage family and on sunny days its leaves release a warm, spicy scent.

GOES WELL WITH . . .

FLOWERS *Anemone* × *hybrida* 'Königin Charlotte' (windflower) *Echinacea pallida* (pale coneflower), *Salvia nemorosa* 'Caradonna' (meadow sage), *Sedum* 'Matrona' (ice plant)
GRASSES *Panicum virgatum* 'Shenandoah' (switch grass)

PERSICARIA

BOTANICAL NAME *Persicaria amplexicaulis*
COMMON NAME Bistort, knotweed
FAMILY Polygonaceae
WHY GROW IT?
  Tapering spikes; happy in shade; flowers
  from midsummer to the first frost.
BEST CULTIVAR
  P. amplexicaulis 'September Spires',
  'Orangofield'
WILDLIFE BENEFITS
  Pollen and nectar source for bees and
  hoverflies, nectar for butterflies.
SIZE Height 1.2m/4ft; spacing 3 per
  square metre/11 square feet

A leafy plant with bright, tapering spikes,
persicaria is a good choice for difficult spots
that don't get many hours of sunshine. It
thrives in the shade and can make a hefty
plant, good for covering the soil and keeping
weeds out. 'Orangofield' has orange spikes
while 'September Spires' is pink.

GOES WELL WITH . . .
FLOWERS *Astrantia* 'Roma'
(masterwort), *Eryngium* × *tripartitum*
(sea holly), *Helenium* 'Rubinzwerg'
(autumn daisy), *Sanguisorba officinalis*
'Red Buttons' (burnet)
GRASSES *Deschampsia cespitosa*
'Goldtau' (tufted hair grass), *Stipa
tenuissima* (feather grass)

*Persicaria
amplexicaulis
'September
Spires'*

GOES WELL WITH . . .

FLOWERS *Knautia macedonica* (scabious), *Salvia verticillata* 'Purple Rain' (whorled clary), *Agastache* 'Blackadder' (giant hyssop)

GRASSES *Panicum virgatum* 'Rehbraun' (switch grass), *Sesleria autumnalis* (autumn moor grass)

PHLOMIS

BOTANICAL NAME *Phlomis russeliana*,
P. tuberosa

COMMON NAME Jerusalem sage,
Turkish sage

FAMILY Lamiaceae

WHY GROW IT?
Whorls of flowers from summer to
early autumn; poker-straight stems;
robust seedheads.

BEST CULTIVAR
P. tuberosa 'Amazone' AGM

WILDLIFE BENEFITS
Pollen and nectar source for
bumblebees; winter homes for
hibernating bees, ladybirds, hoverflies,
lacewings and their larvae.

SIZE Height 90cm/36in; spacing 4 per
square metre/11 square feet.

ABOVE *Phlomis russeliana*
OPPOSITE *Phlomis tuberosa* 'Amazone'

Phlomis produces its flowers in bold whorls on straight, upright stems. It's one of the best plants to choose for a strong vertical accent. The tiers of flowers are spaced along the flower stalks, making them look very architectural. Phlomis can grow quite vigorously and makes a solid clump.

The rings of flowers are made up of small florets that each have a lip and a hood. The lip acts as the landing platform for bumblebees, which are the only bees big and heavy enough to trigger the floret to open. When a bee visits the flowers, the anthers dip and deposit a blob of pollen on the bee's back that's perfectly placed for pollinating the other blooms.

Phlomis is a good match for knautia. Its strong stems provide support for the knautia's whippy frame and the two plants knit together, the neat round flowers of the knautia echoing the the phlomis whorls. I also like it with agastache spikes, which emphasize its upward shape.

Phlomis is a four-season plant with stunning, long-lasting winter seedheads. They have the same knobbled shape as the plant in summer and are very dark in colour. They look magical dusted with frost or snow and are very robust.

SALVIA

LEFT *Salvia nemorosa* 'Caradonna'
OPPOSITE *Salvia* 'Nachtvlinder'

BOTANICAL NAME *Salvia nemorosa*, *S. × sylvestris, S. verticillata*

COMMON NAME Meadow sage

FAMILY Lamiaceae

WHY GROW IT?
Long flowering season from early summer to mid-autumn; bee-blue flowers.

BEST CULTIVARS
S. 'Amistad', *S.* 'Nachtvlinder', *S. nemorosa* 'Caradonna' AGM, *S. × sylvestris* 'Viola Klose', *S. verticillata* 'Purple Rain'

WILDLIFE BENEFITS
Flowers jam-packed with pollen and nectar for bees and hoverflies, nectar source for butterflies.

SIZE Height 0.6–1.2m/2–4ft; spacing 5 per square metre/11 square feet.

The brilliant blue flowers of salvias are sometimes described as 'bee-blue'. Because bees can see ultraviolet light, the electric blues and purples of salvias are easy for them to spot. Other bee-blue plants include *Eryngium* (sea holly), *Agastache* (giant hyssop) and *Perovskia* (Russian sage). Bee-blue flowers often have ultraviolet markings on their petals that are invisible to us but look like street furniture to bees – chevrons and arrows guiding them to the nectar inside. When a bee crawls inside one of salvia's small trumpet-shaped blooms, the weight of the bee activates a trigger that makes the stamens in the flower curl down and deposit a blob of pollen on its back that's perfectly positioned to pollinate other flowers.

Salvia is an upright spike with small flowers dotted up and down strong, narrow stems. The florets are spaced widely apart on each stem, which makes the plants look airy and light. 'Caradonna' is a deep violet-purple with black stems. Its flowers open from pretty criss-crossed buds that decorate the garden in spring almost as much as the flowers do in summer. It's the plant to go to for the darkest, most purple hue. A group of two or three makes an inky pool of colour. It's good with other blue and purple spikes, including other salvias. Because the plants' energy is focused on growing up, rather than out, they make good companions that don't crowd others out. 'Viola Klose' is a brighter purple that's great with 'Caradonna'. 'Amethyst' is a good choice for paler, more pink flowers.

'Amistad' is a tall salvia with twisting, twirling stems that grow to more than 1m/3¼ft tall. It's a more branched and bushy plant than the other salvias, with bigger leaves and flowers.

'Purple Rain' is a more lax salvia with whorls of lilac-purple flowers and pretty felty leaves.

It is best grown with plants that give it some support. Otherwise it has a tendency to flop out with all its flowers round the edge. Try phlomis or verbena.

All salvias are hard-working plants. They bloom for weeks from early summer and then, after a bit of a lull, have a second flush. If you like, you can hurry the lull along and encourage further flowers by cutting off the faded spikes.

GOES WELL WITH . . .
FLOWERS *Geranium* 'Brookside' (cranesbill), *Nepeta racemosa* 'Walker's Low' (catmint), *Rudbeckia occidentalis*
GRASSES *Stipa tenuissima* (feather grass), *Molinia caerulea* subsp. *caerulea* 'Moorhexe' (purple moor grass)

STACHYS

Stachys officinalis 'Hummelo'

BOTANICAL NAME *Stachys officinalis*, *S. byzantinus*
COMMON NAME Betony, lamb's ears
FAMILY Lamiaceae
WHY GROW IT?
  Long-lasting flower spikes from early summer to early autumn; pointed seedheads.
BEST CULTIVAR
  S. officinalis 'Hummelo'
WILDLIFE BENEFITS
  Pollen and nectar source for bees, nectar source for butterflies; nest-building materials for the wool carder bee in *S. byzantinus*.
SIZE Height 50cm/20in; spacing 5 per square metre/11 square feet.

The name 'stachys' originates from the Greek word 'stachus', which means spike, and all stachys have vertical stems of flowers. *Stachys officinalis* is a neat, upright plant with green leathery leaves lower down on the stems. The flowers are all at the tips of the stalks and are like bottlebrushes in purple and pink. It is a popular plant with bees and other pollinators that love its tiny trumpet blooms. My favourite cultivar is 'Hummelo', bred by Piet Oudolf, the pioneer of new perennial planting, who named it after the Dutch village where he lives.

For a hot, sunny spot, *Stachys byzantinus*, known as lamb's ears, is hard to beat. It grows in the wild in Turkey and Iran and every leaf, stalk and flower bud is covered in a silvery, velvety down that protects the plant from the heat of the sun. Its leaves are wonderfully soft and thick, looking as if they have been cut out from pieces of felt – it's impossible not to stroke them. *S. byzantinus* flowers in small whorls of pink and purple but it's mainly grown for its foliage. You might spot a wool carder bee on the plant in summer plucking or 'carding' the tiny leaf hairs to take away and use to build its nest.

GOES WELL WITH . . .

FLOWERS *Salvia verticillata* 'Purple Rain' (meadow sage), *Nepeta racemosa* 'Walker's Low' (catmint), *Perovskia* 'Blue Spire' (Russian sage), *Echinacea purpurea* 'White Swan' (coneflower)
GRASSES *Deschampsia cespitosa* 'Goldtau' (tufted hair grass)

VERONICASTRUM

With tall, architectural stems whorled with upward spikes, veronicastrum is hard to beat for height and structure in late summer. It grows to 1.5m/5ft tall with tapering spikes of flowers that look like candelabra.

Veronicastrum works well with other flowers held on high, clear stems that let the light through. It's good with sanguisorba's scattered burrs or anemones that grow to a similar height, with neat, round buttons for a contrast of shape. It is also good with tall grasses such as miscanthus, or panicum with its gauzy flowers.

Veronicastrum is a mecca for bees, hoverflies, butterflies and moths. The flowers open in succession, making a pretty two-tone effect and keeping the insects coming back day after day, as more pollen and nectar becomes available.

At the end of autumn the flowers disappear but the stems keep their candelabra shape, making elegant bronze spires that pierce the winter sky.

Veronicastrum virginicum 'Album'

BOTANICAL NAME *Veronicastrum virginicum*

COMMON NAME Culver's root

FAMILY Plantaginaceae

WHY GROW IT?
Tall, architectural form; late flowers from midsummer to early autumn.

BEST CULTIVAR
V. virginicum 'Album' AGM

WILDLIFE BENEFITS
Plentiful pollen and nectar for bees, nectar for butterflies.

SIZE Height 1.5m/5ft; spacing 5 per square metre/11 square feet.

GOES WELL WITH . . .

FLOWERS *Anemone hupehensis* 'Hadspen Abundance' (windflower), *Sanguisorba officinalis* 'Red Buttons' (burnet), *Thalictrum delavayi* 'Album' (meadow rue)

GRASSES *Miscanthus sinensis* (Chinese silver grass), *Panicum virgatum* 'Shenandoah' (switch grass)

Dots

DOTS ARE POINTS OF SHAPE AND COLOUR: TIGHT, BRIGHT BUTTONS, SMALL CUPS, CURVED, COLOURFUL SAUCERS AND DAISY FLOWERS WITH ROUND CENTRES.

The predominant shape of a dot flower is a circle. Echinacea, helenium and rudbeckia all look like large daisies, with a ring of colourful petals around a central boss. The plants spend the first part of summer growing as tall as they can before they flower, producing one neat bloom atop every stalk. In the wild we find them in prairie meadows bobbing high above the other plants, like full stops, hoping to be the first to grab the attention of pollinators that fly past.

Plants such as knautia, dianthus and geranium have multiple small flowers. The greater proportion of stem and leaf to flower means the blooms stand out and make spots of colour. They may be held high on a scaffold of stems to make a haze, or cover leafy mounds that hug the soil.

Dots mix well with umbels, spikes and flatheads. A group of daisy flowers will grow to the same height as a sedum or a shorter achillea but with a contrasting shape at the top. Taller dots on long stems will add weight to gauzy panicles and mingle happily with grasses, while an echinacea makes a point above a repeating spike.

ABOVE *Knautia macedonica*
OPPOSITE *Helenium* 'Moerheim Beauty'

ANEMONE

Anemone × *hybrida* 'Robustissima'

BOTANICAL NAME *Anemone hupehensis, Anemone × hybrida*

COMMON NAME Japanese anemone, windflower

FAMILY Ranunculacae

WHY GROW IT?
Robust flowers from late summer to late autumn; cotton-wool seedheads.

BEST CULTIVARS
A. hupehensis var. *japonica* 'Pamina' AGM, *A. hupehensis* 'Hadspen Abundance' AGM, *A. × hybrida* 'Honorine Jobert' AGM, *A. × hybrida* 'Königin Charlotte' AGM, *A. × hybrida* 'Robustissima'

WILDLIFE BENEFITS
Pollen and nectar source for bees and hoverflies, nectar source for butterflies; fluffy seedheads for nest-builders.

SIZE Height 1–1.5m/3¼–5ft; spacing 6 per square metre/11 square feet.

With round, saucer-shaped flowers on tall, straight stems, anemones are fantastic autumn flowers. They bejewel the garden with their shimmering colours, each flower with a shining yellow eye. In my first garden I found out how robust they were; they didn't match my plans and I tried to dig them out. They won and I lost, but in the end we were both winners, as now I love them.

Coming in cherry pink, sugar pink or white, anemones have such pretty colours; and they are resilient little blooms, happy to be buffeted by wind and rain. The paler flowers often have deep plum markings on the back that you can see when they blow and bob about.

Anemones pair well with late summer actaeas for a contrast of shape, one round, one bottlebrush. The colours of their petals are pretty with the bronze leaves of actaeas. They are also good with gauzy, hazy plants like foeniculum or the fronds of deschampsia grasses, where their flowers really pop.

In early winter anemone flowers evolve into fluffy seedheads, like balls of cotton wool atop their narrow stems.

GOES WELL WITH . . .

FLOWERS *Actaea simplex* 'James Compton' (bugbane), *Foeniculum vulgare* 'Purpureum' (bronze fennel)

GRASSES *Deschampsia cespitosa* 'Goldtau' (tufted hair grass)

ASTER

BOTANICAL NAME *Symphyotrichum,
Eurybia, Doellingeria, Aster*

COMMON NAME Aster, Michaelmas daisy

FAMILY Asteraceae

WHY GROW IT?

Good for shady spots; starry flowers
from late summer to early autumn.

BEST SPECIES & CULTIVARS

Symphyotrichum cordifolius (syn.
Aster cordifolius) 'Little Carlow',
Symphyotrichum novae-angliae (syn.
Aster novae-angliae) 'Violetta', *Eurybia* ×
herveyi (syn. *Aster macrophyllus*
'Twilight'), *Doellingeria umbellata* (syn.
Aster umbellatus)

WILDLIFE BENEFITS

Composite flowers that are a pollen and
nectar source for bees and hoverflies
and a nectar source for butterflies.

SIZE Height 90cm/36in; spacing 5 per
square metre/11 square feet.

Symphyotrichum novae-angliae 'Violetta'

Asters bloom during the last days of summer
with a flash of colour, every flower dotted in
the middle with a lemon eye. Good for a tricky
spot that doesn't get hours of sunshine, they
are plants that like a challenge. So, it seems,
do taxonomists, who in recent years have
reclassified many plants in the *Aster* genus
in order to reduce its huge size – at one time
it contained 500 plants. For a while you may
find the ones listed here under other names
still labelled as *Aster* at garden centres.

Asters such as *Symphyotrichum cordifolius*
'Little Carlow' pick up the inky tones of
autumn as the first seedheads appear in the
garden. Asters can be decidedly frothy – not
a bad thing, especially later in the year – and
work well with starker silhouettes. A purple
aster will bring out the plum hues in a sedum,
the pink in a deschampsia and the bronze tint
in an actaea leaf. *S. novae-angliae* 'Violetta'
does this, with bright violet flowers. Planting a
small-flowered aster such as *Eurybia* × *herveyi*
or *Doellingeria umbellata* with grasses brings
out their wildness.

GOES WELL WITH . . .

FLOWERS *Actaea simplex* 'James
Compton' (bugbane), *Helenium*
'Moerheim Beauty' (autumn daisy),
Sedum 'Matrona' (ice plant)

GRASSES *Molinia caerulea* subsp.
caerulea 'Moorhexe' (purple moor grass),
Sesleria autumnalis (autumn moor grass)

CIRSIUM

Cirsium rivulare 'Atropurpureum'

BOTANICAL NAME *Cirsium rivulare*
COMMON NAME Plume thistle
FAMILY Asteraceae
WHY GROW IT?
Bright thistle flowers from early summer to early autumn; gives height in the border.
BEST CULTIVARS
C. rivulare 'Atropurpureum', *C. rivulare* 'Trevor's Blue Wonder'
WILDLIFE BENEFITS
Pollen and nectar source for bees and hoverflies, nectar source for butterflies.
SIZE Height 1.5m/5ft; spacing 2 per square metre/11 square feet.

Just like a wild thistle, the leaves of *Cirsium rivulare* are jagged with sharp teeth and its flowers are upright tufts in criss-cross cups at the tips of tall stems. The brilliant colours of the cultivated varieties coupled with its wild nature makes it an exciting plant to grow. It really is the best of both worlds – spikiness matched with colour.

Despite its wild appearance, this is a well-behaved plant. It grows from a central point and marks its space in the soil, often developing some breadth. It doesn't seed about. Cirsium is always very busy with bees when in flower, but later doesn't have the best seedheads; the seeds are fluffy but don't last long.

GOES WELL WITH . . .

FLOWERS *Sanguisorba officinalis* 'Red Buttons' (burnet), *Astrantia* 'Hadspen Blood' (masterwort), *Salvia nemorosa* 'Caradonna' (meadow sage), *Foeniculum vulgare* 'Purpureum' (bronze fennel)
GRASSES *Deschampsia cespitosa* 'Goldtau' (tufted hair grass)

DIANTHUS

BOTANICAL NAME *Dianthus carthusianorum, D. cruentus*

COMMON NAME Wild carnation, field pink

FAMILY Caryophyllaceae

WHY GROW IT?
Colour pop, subtle scent; flowers from early summer to early autumn.

WILDLIFE BENEFITS
Dianthus carthusianorum is a nectar source for butterflies; *D. cruentus* is a pollen and nectar source for bees, butterflies and hoverflies.

SIZE Height 50cm/20in; spacing 5 per square metre/11 square feet.

Dianthus cruentus

Wild dianthus are a million miles away from the frilly carnations of supermarket bouquets. *Dianthus carthusianorum* (German pink) and *D. cruentus* are a must for spots of brilliant cerise that pop and punctuate the garden. The former has small blooms atop wiry stems, looking as though they are suspended in mid-air, bobbing and weaving about, while the latter has a ball of flowers. As dusk falls, their colours glow. Their skinny stems and grassy foliage belie a robust character; tough plants, they flower for ages and stay upright in all kinds of weather.

Because of their grassy leaves, dianthus can be planted close to other plants, intermingling with them and not blocking their light. The flowers look beautiful threading through stipa grasses or among echinacea flowers.

The flowers are simple and popular with pollinators. *D. carthusianorum* is pollinated by butterflies. The pollen collects on their long legs as they rest on the petals and unfold their proboscis to drink the nectar in the middle of the flower. *D. cruentus* is pollinated by both butterflies and bees.

GOES WELL WITH . . .

FLOWERS *Astrantia* 'Hadspen Blood' (masterwort), *Salvia nemorosa* 'Caradonna' (meadow sage), *Nepeta racemosa* 'Walker's Low' (catmint)

GRASSES *Briza media* (lesser quaking grass), *Stipa tenuissima* (feather grass)

ECHINACEA

People often think of echinacea when they have a cold or a bout of the flu, but echinaceas are also lovely plants to grow.

They look like the sort of flower a child might draw, with a straight, upright stem, a round centre and a ring of petals. Like helenium and rudbeckia, echinacea consists of composite flowers. What we think of as the petals are 'ray florets'.

Echinaceas bloom in midsummer. The shape of the flower centres gives the common name of 'coneflower'; they start rounded but point upwards as the flowers mature, eventually becoming quite pronounced. Their open faces make them popular with bees and butterflies as the petals (ray florets) create a landing platform on the way to the middle of the flower. Bees love them – it's not unusual to see several sharing one flowerhead – and they are also a favourite of butterflies, which rest their legs on the edge as they sip the nectar in the middle.

Echinacea pallida is the the wild-at-heart coneflower. It grows to over 1m/3¼ft tall and is one of my favourite flowers, with a plum centre and narrow, drooping, pale purple ray florets. Graceful and elegant, its tall stem reflects its North American prairie heritage, where it grows wild amid longer grasses. I love it popping up here and there in the garden, mingling with other tall flowers.

Echinacea purpurea 'White Swan' has white ray florets tinged with green, with a yolk-yellow middle. I like it planted with 'Happy Star' – which is similar but flatter – together with sedum and miscanthus. Both cultivars have stout stems and pale flowers with bold shapes.

BOTANICAL NAME *Echinacea pallida, E. purpurea*

COMMON NAME Coneflower

FAMILY Asteraceae

WHY GROW IT?
Daisy flowers from early summer to early autumn; bobble seedheads.

BEST CULTIVARS
E. purpurea 'Happy Star', *E. purpurea* 'White Swan'

WILDLIFE BENEFITS
Composite flowers that are a pollen and nectar source for bees and hoverflies and a nectar source for butterflies.

SIZE Height 1m/3¼ft; spacing 6 per square metre/11 square feet.

Some of the more colourful echinaceas last for only 3–4 years in the garden, and you may suddenly notice one summer that they're not there any more. (Adding a handful of grit to their holes at planting time is said to make them last a bit longer.) *Echinacea pallida*, however, is much more reliable. It will happily scatter its seeds about, too. The seedlings grow up to be 'true' flowers that are identical to the original plant.

OPPOSITE *Echinacea purpurea*

GOES WELL WITH . . .

FLOWERS *Perovskia* 'Blue Spire' (Russian sage), *Sedum* 'Matrona' (ice plant), *Salvia nemorosa* 'Caradonna' (meadow sage)

GRASSES *Stipa tenuissima* (feather grass), *Miscanthus sinensis* (Chinese silver grass)

Echinops has the same
round shape in bud, flower
and seedhead.

ECHINOPS

BOTANICAL NAME *Echinops ritro*
COMMON NAME Globe thistle
FAMILY Asteraceae
WHY GROW IT?
Perfectly round brilliant blue flowers from mid- to late summer; long-lasting drumstick seedheads.
BEST CULTIVAR
E. ritro 'Veitch's Blue'
WILDLIFE BENEFITS
Pollen and nectar for bees and hoverflies; nectar for butterflies; winter homes in the hollow stems for hibernating bees, ladybirds, hoverflies, lacewings and their larvae.
SIZE Height 1.2m/4ft; spacing 3 per square metre/11 square feet.

Echinops ritro

The thistle heritage of echinops shows up in its prickly green leaves, hollow stem and long tap root. It's a tall plant that's quite solid and a bit ungainly, so it's definitely one that's best grown surrounded by other plants. What it lacks in the awkward shape of the plant as a whole it makes up for with its striking flowers, which are brilliant blue and perfectly spherical, borne singly on the stalks.

Echinops works well planted with eryngium, which matches it for height and shape. They both have chunky upright stalks and tight, geometric flowers and their tap roots mean they make a neat clump. Echinops is also a good match for achillea, the flatheads creating a sharp contrast of shape. The seedheads echo the shape of the flowers and last a long time in the garden.

GOES WELL WITH . . .

FLOWERS *Agastache* 'Blackadder' (giant hyssop), *Echinacea pallida* (pale coneflower), *Eryngium agavifolium* (sea holly), *Salvia* × *sylvestris* 'Viola Klose', *Salvia verticillata* 'Purple Rain' (meadow sage)
GRASSES *Sesleria autumnalis* (autumn moor grass), *Stipa gigantea* (golden oats)

GERANIUM

Geranium 'Azure Rush'

BOTANICAL NAME *Geranium*
COMMON NAME Cranesbill, hardy geranium
FAMILY Geraniaceae
WHY GROW IT?
  Flowers from late spring to mid-autumn; suppresses weeds.
BEST CULTIVARS
  G. 'Ann Folkard' AGM, *G.* 'Azure Rush', *G.* 'Brookside' AGM, *G.* × *oxonianum* 'Rose Clair'
WILDLIFE BENEFITS
  Nectar source for bumblebees and butterflies.
SIZE Height 30cm/12in; spacing 3 per square metre/11 square feet.

People often use the name geranium to describe the brightly coloured flowers that are a familiar sight on windowsills, but these are, in fact, correctly pelargoniums. True geraniums are hardy plants that – unlike pelargoniums – are happy to spend the winter outside. They have neat geometric flowers, usually blue, pink or white, and leafy green foliage.

There are hundreds of different geranium cultivars to choose from, varying mostly according to the colour of their flowers. Try *G.* 'Brookside' for blue, *G.* 'Azure Rush' for pale blue and G. 'Ann Folkard' or *G.* × *oxonianum* 'Rose Clair' for the best magenta flowers. Many geraniums have a black splotch in the middle and whiskers marked on their petals to guide pollinators inside.

Geranium are good 'filler' plants, swiftly filling their space with a mound of leaves that make a foil for taller flowers and keep weeds in check. The small flowers are dotted amid the foliage.

GOES WELL WITH . . .

FLOWERS *Nectaroscordum siculum* (Sicilian honey garlic), *Salvia nemorosa* 'Amethyst' (meadow sage), *Rudbeckia occidentalis* (western coneflower)
GRASSES *Sesleria autumnalis* (autumn moor grass)

HELENIUM

Heleniums have coppery-orange daisy-like flowers with round bobble centres that bloom in the second half of summer, their warm, earthy colours reflecting long, lazy days in the sun. The middle of each flower is as round as a ball, held at the top of a tall, straight stem, with the petals swirling around it. Helenium is native to the North American prairies, where it spends early summer growing as tall as it can before the flowers open, so it's a good plant to choose for height. 'Moerheim Beauty' has rich red orange petals that bend backwards from a conker brown centre, looking almost like shuttlecocks. 'Rubinzwerg' is smaller and the flowers more red and flatter but with the same pronounced centre; it's a good choice for a small garden. They both have three months of flowers.

A helenium is a composite daisy. The disk florets in the middle open progressively from the outer circumference inwards, and you can often see bees working their way in a ring around the flower, and returning on subsequent days as more pollen becomes available.

When the flowers lose their colour in autumn the bobble of each flower stays at the top of the stalk, making a black full stop which lasts throughout winter.

Helenium 'Moerheim Beauty'

GOES WELL WITH . . .

FLOWERS *Rudbeckia occidentalis* (western coneflower), *Eryngium agavifolium* (sea holly), *Sanguisorba officinalis* 'Red Buttons' (burnet)
GRASSES *Deschampsia cespitosa* 'Goldtau' (tufted hair grass), *Stipa tenuissima* (feather grass)

BOTANICAL NAME *Helenium*
COMMON NAME Sneezeweed, autumn daisy
FAMILY Asteraceae
WHY GROW IT?
Flowers from mid- to late summer; round, bobble seedheads
BEST CULTIVARS
H. 'Moerheim Beauty' AGM, *H.* 'Rubinzwerg'
WILDLIFE BENEFITS
Pollen and nectar source for bees and hoverflies, nectar source for butterflies.
SIZE Height 1.2m/4ft; spacing 6 per square metre/11 square feet.

KNAUTIA

Knautia macedonica

Knautia has crimson colour-pop flowers on skinny stems that knit happily together with other plants. The flowers look like bright buttons, small, neat, round domes that are softly spiked. It's a member of the thistle family and its wild heritage shows up in its proliferation of flowers, sharply toothed leaves and loose, easy style.

Knautia is one of the longest-flowering perennial plants; the first flowers open in early summer and it keeps going until autumn starts. Although each bloom lasts only two weeks they continue to open one after another. They are followed by very pretty seedheads, round, green balls at the tips of the stalks, bobbing in the breeze.

Its brilliantly coloured flowers and its slightly lax habit, its flowers liking to mingle while its roots stay tidily in one place, make it a lovely plant for a small space, ideally in a sunny spot. As it grows bigger it looks wilder and its flowers mingle more easily, but it still doesn't take over. It makes one of my favourite combinations with phlomis, all airiness and light.

GOES WELL WITH . . .

FLOWERS *Phlomis russeliana* (Jerusalem sage, Turkish sage), *Achillea* 'Summerwine' (yarrow), *Salvia verticillata* 'Purple Rain' (meadow sage), *Rudbeckia occidentalis* (western coneflower)
GRASSES *Sesleria autumnalis* (autumn moor grass)

BOTANICAL NAME *Knautia macedonica*
COMMON NAME Crimson scabious
FAMILY Dipsacaceae
WHY GROW IT?
Colour pops on skinny stems; flowers from early summer to early autumn; bobble seedheads.
WILDLIFE BENEFITS
Flowers packed with pollen and nectar for bees, nectar for butterflies.
SIZE Height 1.5m/5ft; spacing 5 per square metre/11 square feet.

RUDBECKIA

Rudbeckia has yellow daisy flowers with pronounced black centres that really stand out. In the wild it grows in prairies and it works well in the garden planted with taller grasses and other prairie plants such as heleniums and echinaceas. It grows as tall as it can in early summer, eventually poking its head above the other flowers, one neat, bright daisy atop every stalk.

Rudbeckia fulgida var. *sullivantii* 'Goldsturm' has big yellow daisies with jet-black eyes and straight stems. *R. triloba* is smaller. *R. occidentalis* is a more unusual rudbeckia. It has the same bold, black centre but no petals (ray florets), and it makes a very striking dot. Try planting it with *Salvia* 'Amistad', which grows to a similar height, or *Eryngium agavifolium*, which repeats its straight stems and round button flowers.

All rudbeckias make a good choice for bees, hoverflies and butterflies, working hard to catch their attention as they fly past. The disk florets in the middle of each flower are tightly packed together, which pollinators love, and they open in concentric rings on consecutive days.

All rudbeckias last well into autumn and winter. They lose their petals, but keep their middles until you cut them off.

Rudbeckia triloba

BOTANICAL NAME *Rudbeckia fulgida, R. occidentalis, R. triloba*

COMMON NAME Black-eyed Susan, western coneflower

FAMILY Asteraceae

WHY GROW IT?
Bobble flowers from early summer to early autumn; long-lasting seedheads on tall stems.

BEST CULTIVAR
Rudbeckia fulgida var. *sullivantii* 'Goldsturm'

WILDLIFE BENEFITS
A pollen and nectar source for bees, hoverflies and lacewings, nectar source for butterflies. Winter homes in the hollow stems for hibernating solitary bees, ladybirds, hoverflies, lacewings and their larvae.

SIZE Height 0.6–1.2m/2–4ft; spacing 3 per square metre/11 square feet.

GOES WELL WITH . . .

FLOWERS *Eurybia* × *herveyi* (aster), *Foeniculum vulgare* 'Purpureum' (bronze fennel), *Helenium* 'Moerheim Beauty' (autumn daisy), *Salvia nemorosa* 'Caradonna'

GRASSES *Deschampsia cespitosa* 'Goldtau' (tufted hair grass), *Stipa tenuissima* (feather grass)

Flatheads

A FLATHEAD IS A FLOWER COMPOSED OF HUNDREDS OF SMALL FLORETS THAT, GROUPED TOGETHER, MAKE A FLAT TOP.

The botanical name for the inflorescence of a flathead is 'corymb', which translates from Latin as 'cluster'. Most flatheads flower in horizontal layers of blooms, with one corymb overlapping the next and making a plane of texture and colour. With one flat top above each straight stem, their bold architecture works well in a small urban space.

Flatheads work well with other flatheads and with plants that echo their texture in different shapes. Because they typically get bigger by growing out from their crowns at soil level, they stick to the spot where they were first placed. Most of their leaves are at the bottom of the plant, so they are good companions to other plants as they don't take all the light.

The arrangement of the flowers – lots of them, packed together and spread out flat like saucers – makes them good news for all kinds of pollinators. Their nectar and pollen is easy to access, and it's not unusual to see several insects vying for space on the same flathead.

Like most perennials, flatheads will flower in the first year if you plant them from a 9cm/ 3½in pot. They are brilliant four-season plants: pretty, early foliage, colourful, architectural flowers and seedheads that make strong silhouettes in autumn and last into winter too.

ABOVE *Sedum* 'Matrona'
OPPOSITE *Achillea millefolium* 'Summerwine'

ACHILLEA

Achillea millefolium 'Credo'

BOTANICAL NAME *Achillea millefolium*

COMMON NAME Yarrow

FAMILY Asteraceae

WHY GROW IT?
Architectural flowers from early summer to late summer.

BEST CULTIVARS
A. millefolium 'Credo', 'Summerwine', 'Terracotta'

WILDLIFE BENEFITS
Massed flowers with pollen and nectar for bumblebees, honeybees and solitary bees; nectar for butterflies; also visited by lacewings, hoverflies, mini encarsia wasps and ladybirds. Also seed for finches and homes for ladybirds in winter.

SIZE Height 0.5–1.5m/20–60in; spacing 5 per square metre/11 square feet.

Achilleas have flat, horizontal inflorescences composed of hundreds of flowers atop straight, bold stems and feathery foliage. They create layers of colour, opening at different times on a single plant to create a pretty mix of tones. Think vanillas and buttery yellows, lemon and golden sunshine or orange and cherry red. The flowers are followed by bold seedheads that last into winter and repeat the shape of the flowers.

Achilleas are a good match for spikes and dots that grow to a similar height; an achillea with a perovskia makes a lovely combination that's architectural but airy, and infused with light. Achilleas also mingle happily with grasses, which highlight the flat shapes of their flowers. *Panicum virgatum* 'Shenandoah' will pick up the plummy tones of 'Summerwine'; or try *Stipa tenuissima*, which is shorter and will ripple around the flowers.

While achilleas can be quite short-lived, growing them on the scratchier, unimproved soil they would find in the wild and watering them less often makes them more reliable.

GOES WELL WITH . . .

FLOWERS *Helenium* 'Rubinzwerg' (autumn daisy), *Perovskia* 'Blue Spire' (Russian sage), *Sedum tetractinum* 'Coral Reef' (ice plant)

GRASSES *Panicum virgatum* 'Shenandoah' (switch grass), *Stipa tenuissima* (feather grass)

OREGANO

'Rosenkuppel' is an ornamental oregano that is a cousin of the edible herb; crush its round, green leaves between your fingers and you'll smell the familiar warm and pungent scent. You can't eat 'Rosenkuppel', but it's a great plant for outside.

Oregano grows by spreading itself out across the soil as a knitted mat of leaves and sending out short stems. Where the stems touch the soil they grow roots and a new shoot pops up. It spreads slowly, and keeps weeds out.

The flowers of 'Rosenkuppel' are pretty rose-pink and the leaves are tinged with plum. Even a very small plant will produce lots of flowers and it's a very popular plant with pollinators. The loose flatheads are close together and easy to get to; bees, hoverflies, moths and all kinds of butterfly like them.

When the flowers fade oregano's winter skeleton is pale and lacy. It looks delicate, but it's very robust and will still be standing at the end of winter.

Oregano is a smaller flathead, and a good choice for a smaller space. I like it with *Eryngium* × *tripartitum* and an upright molinia grass.

Origanum 'Rosenkuppel'

BOTANICAL NAME *Origanum*
COMMON NAME Oregano
FAMILY Lamiaceae
WHY GROW IT?
Rosy flatheads and woven mats of leaves that deter weeds. Flowers from early summer to early autumn, followed by lacy seedheads.
BEST CULTIVAR
O. 'Rosenkuppel'
WILDLIFE BENEFITS
Pollen and nectar for bees and hoverflies, nectar for butterflies. Hibernation spots for ladybirds in winter.
SIZE Height 60cm/24in; spacing 6 per square metre/11 square feet.

GOES WELL WITH . . .
FLOWERS *Achillea* 'Summerwine' (yarrow), *Eryngium* × *tripartitum* (sea holly)
GRASSES *Molinia caerulea* subsp. *caerulea* 'Moorhexe' (purple moor grass)

SEDUM

Sedum 'Matrona', *Molinia caerulea* subsp. *caerulea* 'Moorhexe', *Panicum virgatum* 'Shenandoah' and *Allium atropurpureum* (seedhead)

With fat, waxy leaves, strong stems and flat, chunky flowerheads, sedum is an architectural plant. The flowers are shades of plum, dusky pink or white.

Sedums partner well with spikes. They make a good match with perovskia, knitting

together where they meet but each staying in their spot without taking over, or with grasses that have clear stems and fancy tops, such as molinia and panicum. Because a molinia is a very upright grass and a sedum is a very flat flathead, they make a strong contrast.

Sedums are brilliant for bees, butterflies and hoverflies; they're top of every list of plants that pollinators love but they are of very little interest to slugs and snails. Fantastic four-season plants, they have long-lasting architectural seedheads too.

BOTANICAL NAME *Sedum*

COMMON NAME Ice plant

FAMILY Crassulaceae

WHY GROW IT?
Flowers late summer to mid-autumn; bold silhouette; architectural seedheads

BEST CULTIVARS
S. 'Matrona', *S. tetractinum* 'Coral Reef'

WILDLIFE BENEFITS
Pollen and nectar for bees and hoverflies, nectar for butterflies. Hibernation spots for ladybirds in winter.

SIZE Height 70cm/27in; spacing 5 per square metre/11 square feet

GOES WELL WITH . . .

FLOWERS *Allium cristophii* (ornamental onion), *Perovskia* 'Blue Spire' (Russian sage)

GRASSES *Panicum virgatum* 'Shenandoah' (switch grass), *Molinia caerulea* subsp. *caerulea* 'Moorhexe' (purple moor grass)

Panicles

PANICLES HAVE THOUSANDS OF SMALL FLOWERS THAT SPANGLE A SCAFFOLD OF AIRY STEMS AND MAKE A CLOUD OF COLOUR.

Planting panicles here and there pulls a garden together. They are fantastic for bringing a wash of colour to the garden – and usually some extra height too – but still letting you see what's behind. They look almost transparent.

Their gauziness highlights the solid outlines of other flowers, so they are a good way to add contrast notes to more sturdy shapes.

They include some of the tallest plants in the brilliant and wild garden; sanguisorbas, verbenas and thalictrum all shoot sky-high in a matter of months. Their skinny stems and small flowers make pretty outlines against a blue sky (or even a fence), where their shapes can easily be seen. They capture the energy of seasonal change.

Panicles typically flower later in the year, stealing the show from mid- to late summer. They don't need staking during the autumn winds as the breeze can blow through their almost leafless stems. They often have long-lasting seedheads.

ABOVE *Verbena bonariensis*
OPPOSITE *Sanguisorba officinalis*

SANGUISORBA

With tight, bright burrs on wiry stems, sanguisorba makes a haze of colour that floats above other plants. It's a tall plant, brilliant for height in a new garden with small blooms that make bright spots of colour.

Sanguisorba's narrow stems and small flowers mean you can plant it anywhere and you'll always be able to see the plants behind it because it's almost transparent. Try matching its wine-coloured flowers with coppery heleniums or spikes of veronicastrum that flower at a similar height.

BOTANICAL NAME *Sanguisorba officinalis*
COMMON NAME Burnet
FAMILY Rosaceae
WHY GROW IT?
  Tall but transparent; clouds of colourful flowers from early summer through to early autumn.
BEST CULTIVAR
  S. officinale 'Red Buttons'
WILDLIFE BENEFITS
  Pollen and nectar source for bees and hoverflies, nectar source for butterflies.
SIZE Height 1.2m/4ft; spacing 3 per square metre/11 square feet.

GOES WELL WITH . . .
FLOWERS *Anemone hupehensis* 'Hadspen Abundance' (windflower), *Cirsium rivulare* 'Atropurpureum' (plume thistle), *Helenium* (autumn daisy), *Veronicastrum virginicum* 'Album' (culver's root)
GRASSES *Panicum virgatum* 'Shenandoah' (switch grass)

Sanguisorba officinalis

THALICTRUM

With clouds of airy flowers, like tiny parachutes and pom-poms, thalictrums are brilliant for summer. Hundreds of small blooms spreading from the stems create puffs of colour from midsummer to early autumn.

Thalictrums pair well with other tall, delicate plants. Try them planted with veronicastrum spikes for thousands of small flowers that reach for the sky in contrasting shapes. I like adding fennel to the mix, for a kaleidoscope of panicle, spike and umbel shapes.

'Hewitt's Double' has luminous pink flowers that open from tight, round, purple buds. For white flowers choose 'Album', which has big white buds like pearls. The flowers of 'Album' are heavier so the stems bend a bit, but it captures the softer side of summer.

Thalictrums grow happily in shade, so they are a good choice for a difficult spot. Their lacy leaves are among the first to pop up in spring – and they are not tempting to slugs and snails.

Thalictrum delavayi 'Album'

BOTANICAL NAME *Thalictrum delavayi*

COMMON NAME Meadow rue

FAMILY Ranunculaceae

WHY GROW IT?
Tall, airy clouds of flowers from midsummer to early autumn.

BEST CULTIVARS
T. delavayi 'Album', 'Hewitt's Double' AGM

WILDLIFE BENEFITS
Pollen and nectar source for bees and hoverflies, nectar source for butterflies.

SIZE Height 1m/3¼ft; spacing 5 per square metre/11 square feet.

GOES WELL WITH . . .

FLOWERS *Veronicastrum virginicum* (culver's root), *Foeniculum vulgare* 'Purpureum' (bronze fennel)

GRASSES *Deschampsia cespitosa* 'Goldtau' (tufted hair grass), *Molinia caerulea subsp. caerulea* (purple moor grass)

VERBENA

BOTANICAL NAME *Verbena bonariensis,*
  V. macdougalii
COMMON NAME Verbena
FAMILY Verbenaceae
WHY GROW IT?
  Blue-purple haze of flowers from
  early summer to early autumn; strong
  stems help to keep other neighbouring
  plants upright.
BEST CULTIVAR
  V. macdougalii 'Lavender Spires'
WILDLIFE BENEFITS
  Pollen and nectar source for bees and
  hoverflies, nectar source for butterflies.
SIZE Height 2m/7ft; spacing 5 per
  square metre/11 square feet

Verbena bonariensis has small, violet-blue flowers held at the tips of long, skinny stems It's a tall plant but with a tiny footprint in the soil. As its long, strong stems grow tall quickly but take up very little physical space, it is brilliant for adding lots of height, but still leaving room for other plants. If you want a gentler alternative to the jolting violet of *V. bonariensis*, you might like to try *V. macdougalii* 'Lavender Spires', with its flowers of a gentler lilac colour.

Verbena is loose and airy, and the best way to use it is to crowd a few plants together. The stems interweave and make a purple haze. These plants are great for propping up more lax flowers as their strong stems make a good support that other plants can loll about in. They'll shore up *Knautia macedonica* or *Salvia verticillata* 'Purple Rain' in late summer.

Verbena is a shorter-lived perennial plant. It lasts for 1–2 years but makes itself more reliable by gently resowing its patch. *V. bonariensis* comes 'true' from seed, which means the new seedlings that push through will always be exactly the same as the parent plant.

Verbena's flowers are among the most popular with insect visitors: all kinds of bees, hoverflies and butterflies love the tiny, dense blooms. It's delightful to see a large butterfly balancing precariously at the top of such a tiny flower on a very tall stem, sipping at the nectar inside.

ABOVE LEFT *Verbena bonariensis*
OPPOSITE *Verbena macdougalii* 'Lavender Spires'

GOES WELL WITH . . .

FLOWERS *Perovskia* 'Blue Spire'
(Russian sage)
GRASSES *Stipa gigantea* (golden oats),
Deschampsia cespitosa 'Goldtau'
(tufted hair grass)

Grasses

GRASSES LOOK COOL AND CATCH THE LIGHT, AND THEY COMBINE EASILY AND BEAUTIFULLY WITH OTHER PERENNIALS TO PULL A GARDEN TOGETHER.

Threading your garden with grasses is a good trick. As a rule of thumb, when you're using grasses, more is more. It's difficult to do much with one plant.

Shorter-growing grasses such as *Stipa tenuissima* are good as filler plants. They'll knit together and make a foil for dots, spikes and umbels to grow through. The other plants can rise above them.

Taller grasses gain their height by virtue of their spikes of flowers. Their stems are hollow and like their leaves they contain lignin – a material also found in the bark of trees – which stops them snapping in the wind. *Briza, Deschampsia, Miscanthus, Molinia, Panicum, Pennisetum, Sesleria, Stipa* – though they look very different from each other, grasses all belong to the same family.

Pairing a tall grass with a chunkier plant will emphasize the contrast in shape. Combining plants with different weights, some solid, some airy and light – rather than relying on short-lived contrasts of colour – is key to making a garden that works hard throughout the year.

The sound of grassy leaves rustling is useful for muffling traffic noise if there are busy roads nearby.

ABOVE *Deschampsia cespitosa* 'Goldtau' and *Eurybia × herveyi*
OPPOSITE *Panicum virgatum* 'Rehbraun'

BRIZA

Briza media

BOTANICAL NAME *Briza media*
COMMON NAME Lesser quaking grass
FAMILY Poaceae
WHY GROW IT?
  Short grass; fat buds; flowers from
  late spring to midsummer, followed by
  quivering seedheads.
BEST CULTIVAR
  B.media 'Golden Bee'
SIZE Height 50cm/20in; spacing 6 per
  square metre/11 square feet

Briza media is a grass with bright green leaves
and big buds that hang from skinny stems.
The buds look almost as if they are suspended
in mid-air, like a swarm of hovering bees. By
summer they are replaced by chunky seeds
that gleam and catch the light.
  Briza grows to knee high. Its common name
of 'quaking grass' refers to the way the buds
and later the seeds ripple and shake in the
slightest breeze.

GOES WELL WITH . . .
FLOWERS *Anthriscus sylvestris*
'Ravenswing' (black cow parsley),
Dianthus carthusianorum (German pink),
Astrantia major 'Claret' (masterwort),
Nectaroscordum siculum (Sicilian
honey garlic)
GRASSES *Stipa tenuissima* (feather grass)

DESCHAMPSIA

BOTANICAL NAME *Deschampsia cespitosa*
COMMON NAME Tufted hair grass
FAMILY Poaceae
WHY GROW IT?
Tall and textural; flowers from early to late summer; gauzy seedheads.
BEST CULTIVAR
D. cespitosa 'Goldtau'
WILDLIFE BENEFITS
Winter homes for ladybirds.
SIZE Height 90cm/36in; spacing 5 per square metre/11 square feet

Deschampsia cespitosa 'Goldtau'

Deschampsia has small, pale, feathery flowers. Gauzy, airy and light, it works well planted in a group of two or three that will mesh together to make a translucent haze. Deschampsia catches the sun and twinkles in the light.

The species name *cespitosa* means 'growing in clumps' and *D. cespitosa* starts life as a mound of grassy foliage. Its habit of growing just from the centre of the crown of the plant means it won't move far from the spot where it's first planted.

It works well with solid dots, flatheads and spikes; anemones and actaea that flower at the same time are good partners, their flowers bobbing on narrow stems and at the same height. It's good with helenium too.

When the weather gets colder deschampia's stems and seedheads bleach white. Despite its softness and haze it is a very strong grass that will stand right into winter, losing only the odd stalk.

GOES WELL WITH . . .
FLOWERS *Anemone × hybrida* 'Königin Charlotte' (windflower), *Actaea simplex* 'James Compton' (bugbane), *Eurybia × herveyi* (aster), *Helenium* 'Moerheim Beauty' (autumn daisy)
GRASSES *Molinia caerulea* subsp. *caerulea* 'Moorhexe' (purple moor grass)

MISCANTHUS

Miscanthus sinensis 'Rotfuchs'

BOTANICAL NAME *Miscanthus sinensis*

COMMON NAME Chinese silver grass

FAMILY Poaceae

WHY GROW IT?
Pearly flower tassels on straight stems from late summer to early autumn; cotton-wool seedheads; robust.

BEST CULTIVARS
M. sinensis 'Kleine Fontäne' (AGM), 'Malepartus'

WILDLIFE BENEFITS
Winter homes in the hollow stems for hibernating ladybirds, solitary bees and lacewings; nest-building material; seed for birds.

SIZE Height variable, up to 2m/7ft; spacing 4 per square metre/11 square feet

Miscanthus grasses stand tall and ramrod straight, their stiff stems decorated with tasselled flowers. On windy days the plaited-silk flower strands stream out, fluttering like flags on the stiff poles of their stalks.

Miscanthus makes a bold clump that acts as a shimmering backdrop for flowers such as anemones and sedums. The flowers evolve into fluffy seedheads that are amazingly robust – they'll still be there, blowing in the wind, at the end of winter.

GOES WELL WITH . . .

FLOWERS *Helenium* 'Rubinzwerg' (autumn daisy), *Anemone × hybrida* 'Honorine Jobert' (windflower), *Sedum* 'Matrona' (ice plant)

GRASSES *Molinia caerulea* subsp. *caerulea* 'Moorhexe' (purple moor grass), *Panicum virgatum* 'Rehbraun' (switch grass)

MOLINIA

BOTANICAL NAME *Molinia caerulea* subsp.
caerulea

COMMON NAME Purple moor grass

FAMILY Poaceae

WHY GROW IT?
Upright needle flowers from early
summer to early autumn.

BEST CULTIVAR
M. caerulea subsp. *caerulea* 'Moorhexe'

WILDLIFE BENEFITS
Winter homes for hibernating ladybirds
and beetles.

SIZE Height 1m/3¼ft; spacing 8 per
square metre/11 square feet

Molinia caerulea subsp. *caerulea* 'Moorhexe'

Molinia is a very upright grass with narrow
stalks and needle-like flowers. An inherently
robust grass that grows on heathlands and
mountainsides in the wild, it makes a strong
vertical clump that is good at supporting
other plants.

Molinia works well planted with spikes –
perovskia echoes its shape and height – or
horizontals such as sedum or achillea. It turns
golden in late summer.

GOES WELL WITH . . .

FLOWERS *Allium atropurpureum*
(ornamental onion), *Perovskia* 'Blue Spire'
(Russian sage), *Sedum* 'Matrona'
(ice plant)

GRASSES *Sesleria autumnalis* (autumn
moor grass)

PANICUM

Panicums have panicles of tiny plum flowers that together create a gossamer haze. They are lovely grasses, tall but delicate and light. Dotted among other plants, they tie a medley of shapes together.

They are among the best grasses for capturing the changing colours of the seasons. They have brilliant autumn colour. When the weather turns colder the leaves of 'Shenandoah' go scarlet at the tips, then completely red.

Panicums are robust grasses and their silhouettes last long into the frosts.

GOES WELL WITH . . .
FLOWERS *Achillea* 'Summerwine' (yarrow), *Origanum* 'Rosenkuppel' (oregano), *Phlomis russeliana* (Jerusalem sage, Turkish sage)
GRASSES *Deschampsia cespitosa* 'Goldtau' (tufted hair grass), *Molinia caerulea* subsp. *caerulea* 'Moorhexe' (purple moor grass)

P. virgatum 'Shenandoah', *Molinia caerulea* subsp. *caerulea* 'Moorhexe' and *Deschampsia cespitosa* 'Goldtau'

BOTANICAL NAME *Panicum virgatum*
COMMON NAME Switch grass
FAMILY Poaceae
WHY GROW IT?
Delicate grassy foliage; airy flowers on ultra-thin stems from late summer to mid-autumn, followed by gauzy seedheads; ties a mixture of different flowers together.
BEST CULTIVARS
P. virgatum 'Rehbraun', 'Shenandoah'
WILDLIFE BENEFITS
Small birds like the seeds.
SIZE Height 1.5–2m/5–7ft; spacing 4 per square metre/11 square feet

PENNISETUM

Pennisetum alopecuroides

BOTANICAL NAME *Pennisetum orientale*
COMMON NAME Fountain grass
FAMILY Poaceae
WHY GROW IT?
Fluffy flowers from midsummer
to early autumn.
BEST CULTIVARS
P. alopecuroides, P. orientale 'Tall Tails'
SIZE Height 0.6–1.8m/2–6ft; spacing 5
per square metre/11 square feet

Pennisetum is a grass with fluffy points of flowers. It's quite upright and provides a good contrast for umbels. 'Tall Tails' works well planted with verbena, particularly 'Lavender Spires', as both plants have skinny stalks and long, narrow shapes.

GOES WELL WITH . . .
FLOWERS *Sedum* 'Matrona' (ice plant),
Verbena bonariensis, Verbena macdougalii
'Lavender Spires'
GRASSES *Sesleria autumnalis* (autumn
moor grass)

SESLERIA

BOTANICAL NAME *Sesleria autumnalis*

COMMON NAME Autumn moor grass

FAMILY Poaceae

WHY GROW IT?
Wiry evergreen leaves; flowers from early summer to mid-autumn.

WILDLIFE BENEFITS
Winter homes for ladybirds

SIZE Height 40cm/16in; spacing 5 per square metre/11 square feet

Sesleria is a pale green grass that makes a wiry clump – a stiff grass rather than a billowing one. Its evergreen foliage is topped with pale tufts of flowers. It is a good foil for other plants, threading easily between them.

GOES WELL WITH . . .

FLOWERS *Allium cristophii* (ornamental onion), *Geranium* × *oxonianum* 'Rose Clair' (hardy geranium), *Sedum* 'Matrona' (ice plant)

GRASSES *Deschampsia cespitosa* 'Goldtau' (tufted hair grass)

Sesleria autumnalis

STIPA GIGANTEA

Stipa gigantea

Stipa gigantea is the tallest grass in the brilliant and wild garden, and its long flower spikes are spangled with tiny golden flowers. It's up and off from the end of spring – the only tall grass to flower early in the year. Threading *S. gigantea* among the other plants in a garden and repeating it in different spots is a popular garden designer's trick. It pulls a medley of different plants together.

Unlike all the other grasses, *S. gigantea* is best planted on its own, with a bit of space around so you can appreciate its shape. You can then repeat it a few times in other spots.

It works well with more weighty flowers. Try it with the dots of composite daisies such as heleniums and rudbeckias, which grow to half its height and share its warm golden hues. And sanguisorbas and verbenas will weave happily around it and are almost as tall.

From the middle of summer it develops seeds where the flowers once were. Held up high, they catch the light when the late summer sun streams through, and last all winter.

BOTANICAL NAME *Stipa gigantea*

COMMON NAME Golden oats

FAMILY Poaceae

WHY GROW IT?
Tall but transparent; flowers from late spring to midsummer; architectural seedheads; evergreen

WILDLIFE BENEFITS
Winter homes in the hollow stems for hibernating bees, ladybirds, hoverflies, lacewings and their larvae.

SIZE Height 2.5m/8ft; spacing 1 per square metre/11 square feet

GOES WELL WITH . . .

FLOWERS *Allium cristophii* (ornamental onion) *Helenium* 'Moerheim Beauty' (autumn daisy), *Rudbeckia triloba* (black-eyed Susan), *Sanguisorba officinalis* 'Red Buttons' (burnet), *Verbena bonariensis*

GRASSES *Pennisetum orientale* 'Tall Tails' (fountain grass)

STIPA TENUISSIMA

Stipa tenuissima is a short grass with lots of very fine, bright green leaves. It's one of the first to shoot in spring and it will still be around at the end of the winter, bleached to blonde by the colder weather. The stalks have pale, feathery tops that give smudges of colour. It makes a gauzy, airy fuzz.

A patch of *S. tenuissima* next to a taller grass or other tall plants will add some ups and downs to your garden. It's a brilliant foil for architectural flowers such as nectaroscordum or, later in the year, echinacea and rudbeckia. It pulls different shapes of flowers together while letting them have some space and not competing with them too much.

Stipa can seed about a bit, which is a good thing. Popping up here and there, it's great for knitting a garden together and making it feel one whole space. The seedlings will have the characteristics of the original grass. Because this stipa doesn't grow too tall it's a very useful filler plant.

Stipa tenuissima

GOES WELL WITH . . .

FLOWERS *Nectaroscordum siculum* (Sicilian honey garlic), *Echinacea pallida* (pale coneflower), *Helenium* 'Moerheim Beauty' (autumn daisy)
GRASSES *Deschampsia cespitosa* 'Goldtau' (tufted hair grass), *Panicum virgatum* 'Shenandoah' (switch grass)

BOTANICAL NAME *Stipa tenuissima*
COMMON NAME Mexican feather grass
FAMILY Poaceae
WHY GROW IT?
  Short grass with fuzzy texture, useful for linking different plants; flowers from early summer to early autumn.
BEST CULTIVAR
  Stipa tenuissima 'Pony Tails'
WILDLIFE BENEFITS
  Winter homes for hibernating ladybirds and beetles.
SIZE Height 60cm/24in; spacing 6 per square metre/11 square feet

Bulbs, corms & tubers

IT'S AMAZING THAT SUCH A WORLD OF WONDER CAN GROW FROM SUCH SMALL, DRY BEGINNINGS.

Planting bulbs, corms or tubers is an exciting thing to do. Firework alliums, velvety tulips, candelabra nectaroscordums – all start life as dry brown plant material.

Bulbs, corms and tubers are dormant shoots, stems and roots – packages that contain everything necessary to grow into fully fledged plants as soon as the conditions are right. Tulips, alliums and other bulbs that flower in spring work particularly well in the brilliant and wild garden because at the point at which their needs for water, light and nutrients are highest there are fewer other plants around to compete.

Spring bulbs need to be planted in late autumn and spend the winter underground in the cold and dark. Low temperatures allow the buds to develop inside the bulbs and stimulate gibberellin, a hormone that pulls the leaves and flower stems up to the light in spring. The dark also makes the roots grow, so the bulb is anchored in the soil and can take up the water it requires.

Choosing bulbs is fun, and flicking through a bulb catalogue is a lovely way to spend a wet autumn afternoon. Because most bulbs flower early in the year, you can choose what you like, not necessarily worrying about whether they fit in with the rest of the planting scheme. Having some clashing brights can be an exciting way to start spring. Too often I have chosen the subtler shades and then found that I am in need of a bigger hit of colour after the muted tones of winter.

Plant tulip bulbs in groups, spacing them closely but keeping in mind the eventual size. They'll create pools of colour amidst the new foliage of other plants.

Bulbs such as larger alliums and nectaroscordums can be planted in ones or twos or even scattered across the whole of a smaller garden.

Bulbs are usually planted last in a new garden. If this doesn't fit in with your plans you'll still need to plant them in autumn, but use a plant label as a marker to flag up where you put them, so you don't accidentally dig up a bulb when you are later planting something else. Alliums, nectaroscordums and some tulip bulbs come back every year.

Allium hollandicum 'Purple Sensation'

ALLIUM

Allium cristophii

BOTANICAL NAME *Allium atropurpureum,*
A. cristophii, A. hollandicum,
A. schubertii, A. sphaerocephalon

COMMON NAME Ornamental onion

FAMILY Alliaceae

WHY GROW IT?
Starburst and pompom flowers
from late spring to early summer;
architectural seedheads

BEST CULTIVAR
A. hollandicum 'Purple Sensation''

WILDLIFE BENEFITS
Source of pollen and nectar for bees
and nectar for butterflies; large, robust
flowers for bigger pollinators to land on.

SIZE Height 60cm/24in; spacing 20cm
between bulbs.

With starburst flowerheads atop poker-straight stems, alliums flower at the start of summer. Every flower is a showstopper; thousands of tiny blooms held in orbit around a central point. They make balls, stars and, planted together, lovely ribbons of colour. The flowers last for ages in the garden.

Allium hollandicum 'Purple Sensation' has round flowers the size of tennis balls. It's lovely bobbing above the other plants in your garden as they come into flower. *A. cristophii* is round and bigger, with flowers that can reach 20cm/8in across. They have shorter stems and they are best planted in ones or twos and given some space. *A. schubertii* is the firework allium; its pink and green flowers are the best ones to choose for lasting seedheads. They have the same starburst shapes as the flowers. *A. atropurpureum* has smaller flowers in blackcurrant shades.

Plant allium bulbs 15cm/6in deep in the soil. Their leaves push up before the flowers and can look quite tatty by the time the blooms appear, but it's important not to take them off, because they'll feed the bulbs for the following year. They are low down on the plant, so are easily covered by other foliage.

GOES WELL WITH . . .

FLOWERS *Geranium* × *oxonianum* 'Rose Clair' (hardy geranium), *Nepeta racemosa* 'Walker's Low' (catmint), *Salvia verticillata* 'Purple Rain' (meadow sage)

GRASSES *Deschampsia cespitosa* 'Goldtau' (tufted hair grass), *Stipa tenuissima* (feather grass), *Sesleria autumnalis* (autumn moor grass)

DAHLIA

BOTANICAL NAME *Dahlia*
COMMON NAME Dahlia
FAMILY Asteraceae
WHY GROW IT?
  Whirligig flowers with jewel colours
  from late summer to the first frost.
BEST CULTIVARS
  D. 'Bishop of Llandaff', 'Roxy'
WILDLIFE BENEFITS
  Pollen and nectar source for bees,
  nectar source for butterflies.
SIZE Height 1m/3¼ft; spacing 2 per
  square metre/11 square feet.

Dahlia 'Roxy'

Dahlias are the go-to plants for whirligig flowers. Their blooms can be as big as saucers and shaped like water lilies, cacti or pompoms. Unapologetically chintzy, they are hard to beat for the last hurrah of summer. A scarlet *Dahlia* 'Bishop of Llandaff' hovering amid *Stipa gigantea* on a misty autumn morning is a wonderful sight.

To keep pollinators really happy, single-flowered dahlias are the ones to choose. Also, single flowers are less heavy so don't need staking. They make great cut flowers as the more you snip away the more you will have growing in your garden.

You can buy dahlias as plants in pots, but it's much more thrifty to grow them yourself from tubers; you'll also get a much wider choice of cultivars. A dry tuber looks rather like a hand of fat, sausagey fingers. Plant in late spring as, like bulbs, they need some time underground before they flower. Slugs love dahlia shoots – pick off any you see when the shoots are young, but once the plants get going they'll shrug them off themselves.

I leave dahlia tubers in the soil over winter: they flower in the first year and keep coming back. In areas with cold winters, they will need to be dug up after the first frost has blackened the foliage and stored in a cool frost-free place until late spring.

GOES WELL WITH . . .

FLOWERS *Anemone × hybrida* 'Königin Charlotte' (windflower)
GRASSES *Deschampsia cespitosa* 'Goldtau' (tufted hair grass), *Stipa gigantea* (golden oats)

NECTAROSCORDUM

Nectaroscordum siculum

BOTANICAL NAME *Nectaroscordum siculum*
COMMON NAME Sicilian honey garlic
FAMILY Alliaceae
WHY GROW IT?
   Wild, natural appearance; flowers from late spring to early summer; pointed seedheads.
WILDLIFE BENEFITS
   Pollen and nectar source for bees and hoverflies.
   SIZE Height 1m/3¼ft; spacing 6 per square metre/11 square feet.

Nectaroscordums are wonderful flowers – chandeliers of dangling bell-florets in greenish-white, tinged with plum and pink. They look waxy and quite exotic and work hard in a simple scheme with grasses. Plant nectaroscordum bulbs in autumn and the buds will shoot up in spring. When the flower buds turn papery at the tips of the stalks it means that they are about to burst open. After they have been pollinated, the blooms tilt sharply upwards to resemble the turrets of a castle. The seedheads last throughout winter.

It works well to plant the bulbs in irregular patterns, so the flowers pop up here and there among your other plants. A good way to decide where to place the bulbs is to throw a handful in the air and plant each one exactly where it lands, which gives a random pattern that is tricky to achieve with more careful planting.

For such a pretty flower, nectaroscordum has a very curious smell, a mixture of onions and petrol. The flowers are loved by bees and each floret is large enough for a big bumblebee to crawl completely inside.

GOES WELL WITH . . .

FLOWERS *Anthriscus sylvestris* 'Ravenswing' (Queen Anne's lace), *Astrantia major* 'Claret' (Hattie's pincushion), *Geranium* 'Brookside' (hardy geranium)
GRASSES *Briza media* (lesser quaking grass), *Deschampsia cespitosa* 'Goldtau' (tufted hair grass), *Stipa tenuissima* (Mexican feather grass)

TULIP

Tulips are brilliant for starting the year with a bang and capturing the energy of spring. When most of the activity of other plants is happening below the surface of the soil, tulips are up and off. They bloom in a painter's palette of colours and with the promise of all the good things to come.

Tulips are best planted in groups of at least ten and limited to one or two colours. They really need to be planted in late autumn, as the cold weather stimulates their flowers and also helps to prevent the disease called tulip fire. During the dark days of winter it's lovely to know that they are busily working away underground, sending out roots and preparing for spring.

Tulips are traditionally planted in holes twice as deep as the bulb is tall, but the protection offered by deeper planting (20–30cm/8–12in) can make it more likely that they will come back and flower again. Though species tulips are reliably perennial, not all cultivars are perennial in cooler climates. However, I have found 'Negrita', 'Spring Green', 'White Triumphator' and 'Purissima' to be reliable.

Tulips are a boon for early solitary bees and bumblebee queens. The flowers with simpler shapes are the best ones to choose for pollinators.

Tulipa 'Spring Green'

BOTANICAL NAME *Tulipa*
COMMON NAME Tulip
FAMILY Liliaceae
WHY GROW IT?
　Early flowers give pops of colour.
BEST CULTIVARS
　'Negrita', 'Purissima', 'Spring Green',
　'White Triumphator'
WILDLIFE BENEFITS
　Early pollen and nectar source for
　bumblebee queens and solitary bees.
SIZE Height 45cm/18in; plant in groups
　of 10 or more, 15cm/6in between bulbs.

GOES WELL WITH . . .

FLOWERS Mix and match with other tulips
GRASSES *Stipa tenuissima* (Mexican feather grass)

Differently shaped flowers on strong stems will become decorative seedheads that will make your garden magical in winter.

Winter seedheads

SEEDHEADS ARE STYLIZED VERSIONS OF THE ORIGINAL FLOWERS. CANDELABRA UMBELS, STARBURST ALLIUMS AND KNOTTY BUMPS OF PHLOMIS ON POKER-STRAIGHT STEMS EVOLVE INTO SHOWSTOPPING SILHOUETTES THAT WILL GIVE YOUR GARDEN HEIGHT AND STRUCTURE POST-BLOOM.

Because they are perennial, plants such as these invest their energies in creating strong stems and architectural seed-cases rather than scattering seeds profusely. Unlike annuals that have to start again every year with a new generation of plants, perennials are not in a hurry to create seedlings, and the seeds they do produce are held on sturdy structures in long-lasting shapes. Even after they have passed their traditional best, gleaming white perovskia spikes, flat-top sedums, prickly eryngiums and frothy plumes of miscanthus create a magical autumn and winter show.

Flowers with shapes that last will make your garden look amazing during the coldest, shortest days of the year. Giving your plants a hard life by letting them get on with it naturally rather than feeding or watering them generously will make spiked, round, flat and starburst silhouettes that will continue to decorate your space outside. Backlit by late summer sun or etched in frost, they look beautiful from the windows even when it is too cold to go outside.

Enjoying your plants at every stage in their life cycle rather than only when they are in full bloom is a fantastic way to get to know your garden better and really understand your plants. You'll start to see when it's most important to stop slugs in their tracks (early spring) and which of your plants will produce more flowers if you cut some for the kitchen table (nepeta, salvia, anemone, dahlia and many more). You'll be able to distinguish a valuable seedling from a troublesome weed and recognize when it's the right time to cut back old spent stems in spring. You'll know if a plant needs watering or not and how quickly you can expect it to grow. Enjoying your flowers full circle – shoot, bud, flower and seedhead – makes looking after your garden easy.

Oregano seedheads

TEN PLANTS WITH ARCHITECTURAL STEMS AND SEEDHEADS

Achillea 'Terracotta'
Allium schubertii
Echinacea pallida
Eryngium agavifolium
Perovskia 'Blue Spire'
Phlomis russeliana
Rudbeckia fulgida var.
   sullivantii 'Goldsturm'
Sedum 'Matrona'
Stipa gigantea
Thalictrum delavayi

LEFT Skeletons of *Foeniculum vulgare*
BELOW LEFT *Eryngium eburneum* rimed in frost
BELOW RIGHT *Perovskia* 'Blue Spire'
OPPOSITE The winter heads of asters twinkle like stars.

Combining different shapes, heights and textures is the way to keep a garden interesting long after the colours fade.

Planting

CHOOSING FROM A PALETTE OF PLANTS IS ABOUT MIXING AND MATCHING DIFFERENT SHAPES TO CREATE REPETITION AND CONTRASTS.

Choosing which plants to grow in your new garden is all about creating good combinations. Combine different shapes and use plants that will help each other out.

The most important question to ask yourself when you start to write the plant list for your garden is 'What do I love and want to grow?' Think about the plants that you like best and pinpoint exactly why you like them. Is it their wonderful colours and airy nature? Or the way they move about in the wind? Maybe you know they are a favourite with bees. Choose one plant that you particularly want and use it as the starting point to build your plant list around.

Not every plant on your list needs to be a showstopper – it's important to include some quieter elements. Background plants create a matrix that lets the bold ones shine out.

Smaller plants and grasses are good as background or matrix plants. They are brilliant for bringing a change of rhythm and a different height to your scheme between the showier flowers.

KEEPING IT SIMPLE
The best way to achieve a cohesive design is to limit the number of different plants you have in your garden, with the same shapes and colours repeating again and again. Think about a wild space, where the same flowers appear and reappear in different spots. Including many different flowers can look too busy, especially in a smaller garden, as everything competes for attention. As a guideline, restrict yourself to seven different plants in three different shapes. Repetition is key.

Salvia 'Amistad'

EARLY SUMMER

FRIENDS WITH BENEFITS
Knautia macedonica
• Phlomis russeliana

Phlomis russeliana pairs well with
Knautia macedonica. Whorled up and
down poker-straight stems, the phlomis
flowers echo knautia's dots atop their
whippy stalks. Both flowers are as
round as buttons, brightly coloured and
a similar size. The strong stalks of the
phlomis help knautia reach for the skies.
This is a tall combination that you can
see through and enjoy the plants behind.

EARLY SUMMER

CHEEK BY JOWL
Allium cristophii • Geranium × oxonianum
'Rose Clair' • *Nepeta racemosa* 'Walker's Low'
• Sesleria autumnalis

Nepeta, geraniums and sesleria grass knit
happily together here with a ribbon of
alliums running through. *Nepeta racemosa*
'Walker's Low' and *Allium cristophii* work
well in the same scheme. Although the
flowerheads are different shapes – one
is a spike and the other is round – both
are made up of numerous small flowers.
There's space here too for *Geranium ×
oxonianum* 'Rose Clair' to show off
the neat geometry of its flowers. This
combination will swiftly fill its space but
because the plants all branch from central
points rather than racing off, it won't
spread too much for a small garden.

MIDSUMMER

KALEIDOSCOPE OF SHAPES

Echinacea pallida • *Eryngium agavifolium*
• *Salvia nemorosa* 'Caradonna'

Different flower shapes are used here to make a garden that happily straddles the seasons. *Salvia nemorosa* 'Caradonna' spikes, *Echinacea pallida* dots and *Eryngium agavifolium* umbels grow well together and even after the colours fade their architectural seedheads will echo the shapes of their flowers. As well as the visual attraction they provide, flowers of different shapes attract a range of pollinators too, as some insects are adapted to be able to access the centre of particular plant forms.

EARLY AUTUMN

SHAPE FIRST

Allium atropurpureum (seedhead)
• *Molinia caerulea* subsp. *caerulea*
'Moorhexe' • *Perovskia* 'Blue Spire'
• *Sedum* 'Matrona'

Providing a trinity of flathead, spike and grass, this sedum, perovskia and molinia scheme has contrast as the key. The flat horizontals of *Sedum* 'Matrona' juxtapose perovskia's upward spires and the grass adds an extra vertical. *Allium atropurpureum* will have finished flowering and now its beaded seedheads will pick up the shape and texture of the sedum.

EARLY AUTUMN

EARLY AUTUMN

HEIGHT IS EVERYTHING
Pennisetum orientale 'Tall Tails'
• *Verbena macdougalii* 'Lavender Spires'

Pennisetum's caterpillar spikes are a good match for *Verbena macdougalii* 'Lavender Spires'. Both plants have skinny stalks and long, narrow shapes. They flower at the same time and at the same height, and with scant leaves to interrupt the flowers they weave together easily.

POINTS OF COLOUR
Anemone × *hybrida* 'Hadspen Abundance'
• *Panicum virginatum* 'Shenandoah'
• *Sanguisorba officinalis* 'Red Buttons'

Rosy *Anemone hupehensis* 'Hadspen Abundance' is the star of this dot and panicle scheme. It flowers from midsummer to mid-autumn. The round, velvety flowers are set off by sanguisorba's pinpricks of colour. Airy *Panicum virgatum* 'Shenandoah' adds a lighter note that ripples in the breeze.

EARLY AUTUMN

BOLD BLOCKS
Agastache (seedheads) • *Eryngium yuccifolium*
• *Eurybia* × *herveyi* • *Sesleria autumnalis*

Clean lines and simple shapes make
this layered combination. Blocks of
Eryngium yuccifolium, *Sesleria autumnalis*
and *Eurybia* × *herveyi* grow to different
heights. The agastache that flowered in
summer adds another layer and picks up
the shapes of the other plants.

EARLY AUTUMN

REPEAT, REPEAT
Allium atropurpureum • *Eryngium yuccifolium*
• *Helenium* 'Moerheim Beauty'

Mixing flowers with similar shapes but
different weights creates rhythm. *Allium
atropurpureum*, *Eryngium yuccifolium* and
Helenium 'Moerheim Beauty' take up
different amounts of space; the helenium
flowers grow closely together, eryngiums
are branched and the alliums are widely
apart, one flower per stalk.

Happily knitted together: *Echinops* 'Veitch's Blue' and *Perovskia* 'Blue Spire'

Planting plans

A PLANTING PLAN, SWIFTLY DRAWN, IS AN INVALUABLE DOCUMENT FOR SPARKING CREATIVITY AND CREATING ORDER. IT'S A MAP THAT PLOTS THE WAY TO YOUR OWN WONDERFUL FLOWERY WORLD.

Without a plan, a garden can turn into just a medley of things you like. A piece of paper, a ruler, an eraser, a pencil and some coloured crayons will let you sketch out your ideas, create combinations and plan how to repeat them before picking up a spade or spending any money. It'll probably involve some scribbling and erasing, but a basic sketch can be very quick.

Start by writing a wish list. Flag up your favourite flowers that you want to include no matter what, then pencil in arrows to join up plants that go together. Perhaps they have the same amazing shapes or beautiful colour tones. Mark up effective contrasts, too.

Take an inventory of heights. You want your garden to be immersive – for looking across, through, up at and over. Aim for a mix. Including some tall plants is even more important in a small garden.

With a sharp pencil and a critical eye, refine your list to no more than six or seven must-have plants. This will give plenty of scope for the repetition that is key to making the garden one whole space.

Salvia × *sylvestris* 'Viola Klose'

Drawing a plan is useful for sparking ideas. The whole of your planting plan should fit on a single piece of paper.

Next, draw an outline of your planting area on a piece of paper. A scale of 3cm:1m/1in:3ft works best. The whole plan should fit on to a single sheet, as it's easy to fill a drawing that's too big with excessive detail. Bold lines and shapes are best.

Divide the outline into simple geometric shapes, each to represent a group of a single species. Make some blocks bigger and some smaller, just like the patchworks in a wild plant community. Allocate the plants between the blocks, using every plant in at least two blocks. Think about using plants that echo each other or strongly contrast in adjacent spaces. Also, consider what you will see first when you look out of the windows or come out of the door. If you have a favourite plant or combination you are excited about, place it where you will see it most.

If you own a bigger garden and you are planning two planting areas, use mainly the same plants in both – you might want to take something out or make one new addition from your list.

Ribbons of a single plant that pop up here and there throughout the space are a good way to tie everything together, so add some to your plan. Bulbs such as nectaroscordum or allium work well for this.

When you feel your plan is complete, review it carefully. It can be useful to make a simple sketch of the flower shapes at this stage. Imagine you are standing in front of your garden and looking straight at it, then draw what you will see. Use simple lines to represent the heights and shapes of your plants to give you an overview of how it will look.

Use the planting plans here as a starting point – a source of inspiration and information rather than a fixed design. Trace a plan that you like and make a few copies. Using the same layout, change the pattern of planting, or replace one or more plants with ones you particularly want to include. Try different variations until you feel you have arrived at the best design.

The plans include tips about the elements that particular plants contribute to the design to help you make your own swaps and additions.

Unexpected wild

PLANT LIST

Achillea 'Summerwine'
Achillea 'Terracotta'
Allium hollandicum
    'Purple Sensation'
Eryngium agavifolium
Perovskia 'Blue Spire'
Salvia 'Amistad'
Salvia nemorosa
    'Amethyst'

WHY IT WORKS

This plan uses plants that are all strongly vertical. Planted together, they create a tall garden with some variation in height: *Salvia nemorosa* 'Amethyst' grows to half the height of *S.* 'Amistad', for example, while the eryngium makes tall towers. Flathead achilleas offer a change of shape that lasts into winter with their decorative seedheads.

   This is a scheme that bees will love.

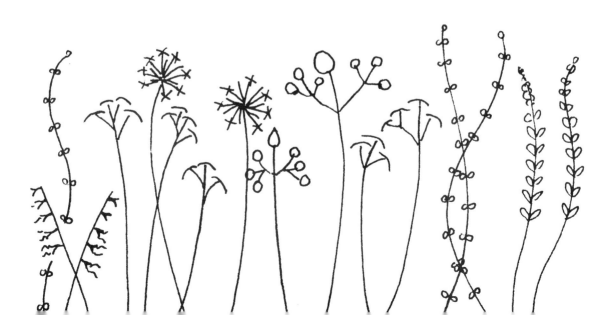

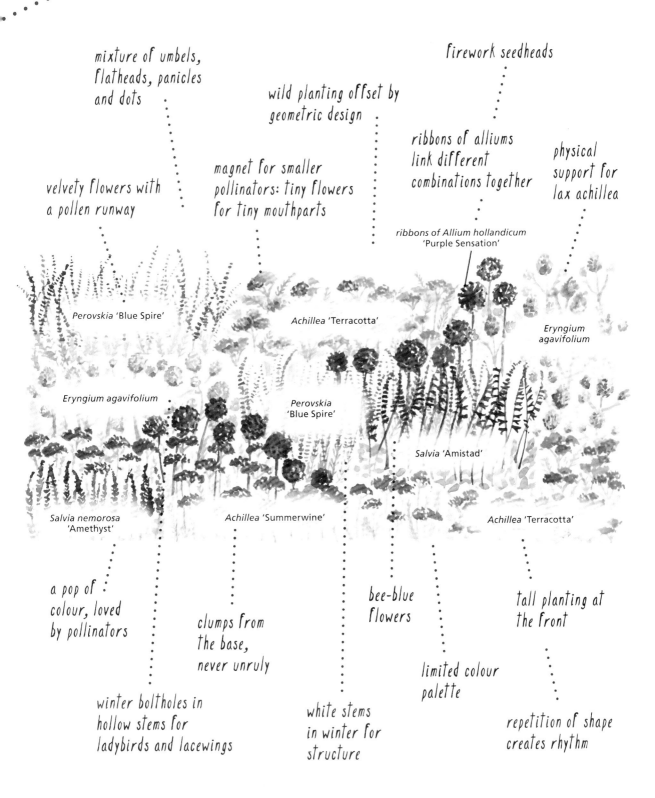

mixture of umbels, flatheads, panicles and dots

firework seedheads

wild planting offset by geometric design

ribbons of alliums link different combinations together

physical support for lax achillea

velvety flowers with a pollen runway

magnet for smaller pollinators: tiny flowers for tiny mouthparts

ribbons of *Allium hollandicum* 'Purple Sensation'

Perovskia 'Blue Spire'

Achillea 'Terracotta'

Eryngium agavifolium

Eryngium agavifolium

Perovskia 'Blue Spire'

Salvia 'Amistad'

Salvia nemorosa 'Amethyst'

Achillea 'Summerwine'

Achillea 'Terracotta'

a pop of colour, loved by pollinators

bee-blue flowers

tall planting at the front

clumps from the base, never unruly

limited colour palette

winter boltholes in hollow stems for ladybirds and lacewings

white stems in winter for structure

repetition of shape creates rhythm

Medley of shapes

PLANT LIST
Actaea simplex 'James Compton'
Anemone hupehensis 'Hadspen Abundance'
Deschampsia cespitosa 'Goldtau'
Foeniculum vulgare 'Giant Bronze'
Tulipa 'Spring Green'

WHY IT WORKS
This plan combines tall plants with flowers and foliage that reach for the skies with lower-growing species that cover the soil with their leaves. The tulips kick things off in spring and are then overtaken by the perennial plants from early summer. Fennel's froth of foliage and the gauzy panicles of the deschampsia grass are punctuated by yellow umbels and later by anemone's saucer flowers. In autumn the actaea has bottlebrush flowers high on soaring stems. All these plants have architectural seedheads that will decorate the garden in winter.

seedheads echo the shapes of the flowers

horizontal stems spread underground to fill gaps

covers the soil and keeps weeds out

pretty after the flowers are over

gives height

makes itself more reliable by gently seeding about

mixture of umbels, spikes and dots

early flowerer

bottlebrush flowers

more solid flowers

more airy flowers

Tulipa 'Spring Green'

Tulipa 'Spring Green'

Deschampsia cespitosa 'Goldtau'

Anemone hupehensis 'Hadspen Abundance'

Foeniculum vulgare 'Giant Bronze'

Actaea simplex 'James Compton'

Anemone hupehensis 'Hadspen Abundance'

Foeniculum vulgare 'Giant Bronze'

Deschampsia cespitosa 'Goldtau'

Actaea simplex 'James Compton'

Deschampsia cespitosa 'Goldtau'

Actaea simplex 'James Compton'

Anemone hupehensis 'Hadspen Abundance'

Tulipa 'Spring Green'

happy company: plants clump from the base and don't spread

late flowerer

leafless stems let light penetrate to the plants below

flowers for more than 12 weeks

repeating the same combinations creates a unified space

a strong vertical shape

long structural season

bold groups of flowers are good news for flying insects

grasses echo a wild place

big groups look contemporary

a pop of colour

Dots and spires

PLANT LIST

Allium atropurpureum
Molinia caerulea subsp.
   caerulea 'Moorhexe'
Perovskia 'Blue Spire'
Sedum 'Matrona'
Sesleria autumnalis

WHY IT WORKS

Thousands of tiny flowers held in various shapes work together in this textural scheme. Allium, sedum and perovskia flower consecutively from mid-spring to early autumn as ball, flathead and spike. Their silhouettes have good contrasts of shape but their textures echo and repeat. Grasses with bare stems and fluffy tips add movement on windier days, as well as variations in height.

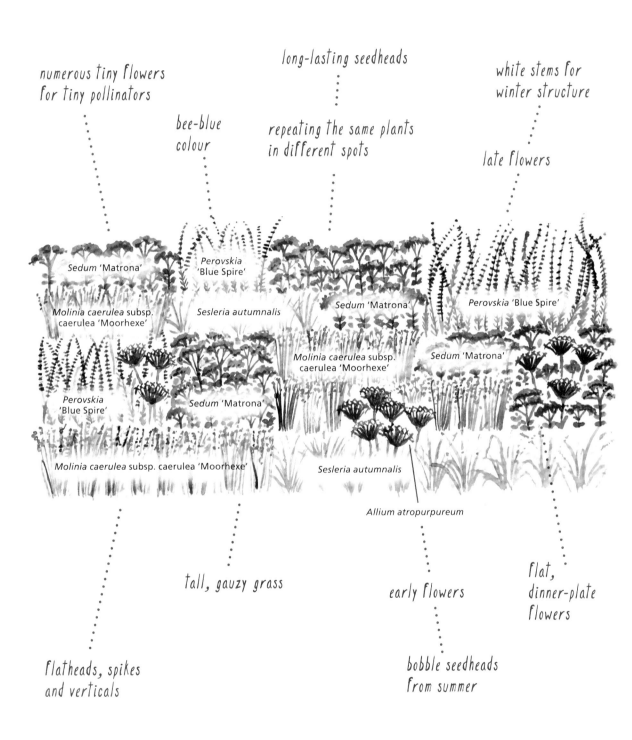

numerous tiny flowers
for tiny pollinators

bee-blue
colour

long-lasting seedheads

repeating the same plants
in different spots

white stems for
winter structure

late flowers

Sedum 'Matrona'

Perovskia
'Blue Spire'

Molinia caerulea subsp.
caerulea 'Moorhexe'

Sesleria autumnalis

Sedum 'Matrona'

Perovskia 'Blue Spire'

Molinia caerulea subsp.
caerulea 'Moorhexe'

Sedum 'Matrona'

Perovskia
'Blue Spire'

Sedum 'Matrona'

Molinia caerulea subsp. caerulea 'Moorhexe'

Sesleria autumnalis

Allium atropurpureum

tall, gauzy grass

early flowers

flat,
dinner-plate
flowers

flatheads, spikes
and verticals

bobble seedheads
from summer

Bobbles and grasses

PLANT LIST

Eurybia × *herveyi* (syn.
  Aster macrophyllus
  'Twilight')
Deschampsia cespitosa
  'Goldtau'
Helenium 'Moerheim
  Beauty'
Rudbeckia triloba
Stipa tenuissima

WHY IT WORKS

Grasses of different heights and weights knit together in this bronze, yellow and copper plan. The deschampsia's low-growing foliage works with the stipa to cover the soil but its flowers match the dots for height. Yellow-flowered rudbeckia and orange helenium give spots of colour and later their seedheads punctuate the grasses as round balls. In autumn asters add a last hurrah with their violet star-shaped flowers.

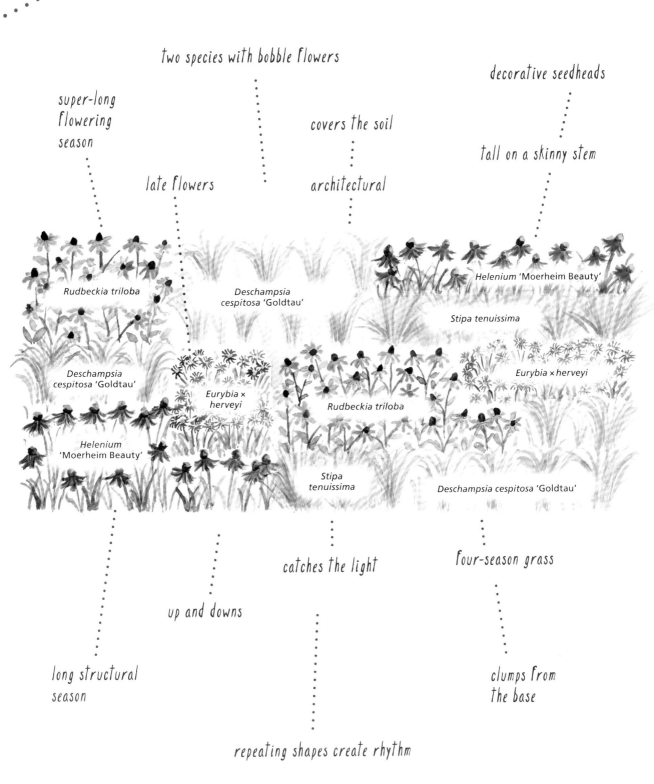

two species with bobble flowers

decorative seedheads

super-long
flowering
season

covers the soil

tall on a skinny stem

late flowers

architectural

Rudbeckia triloba

Deschampsia
cespitosa 'Goldtau'

Helenium 'Moerheim Beauty'

Stipa tenuissima

Deschampsia
cespitosa 'Goldtau'

Eurybia ×
herveyi

Eurybia × herveyi

Rudbeckia triloba

Helenium
'Moerheim Beauty'

Stipa
tenuissima

Deschampsia cespitosa 'Goldtau'

catches the light

four-season grass

up and downs

long structural
season

clumps from
the base

repeating shapes create rhythm

Height is everything

PLANT LIST

Miscanthus sinensis
  'Malepartus'
Rudbeckia triloba
Sanguisorba officinalis
  'Red Buttons'
Verbena bonariensis

WHY IT WORKS

Height is all in this four-season planting plan that's a medley of juxtaposing textures. Verbena is a scaffold of stalks that are spangled with violet flowers. It matches the miscanthus for height but with a pop of colour. Planting in big blocks works well in a small garden. It looks contemporary and allows the shapes of the different plants to shine.

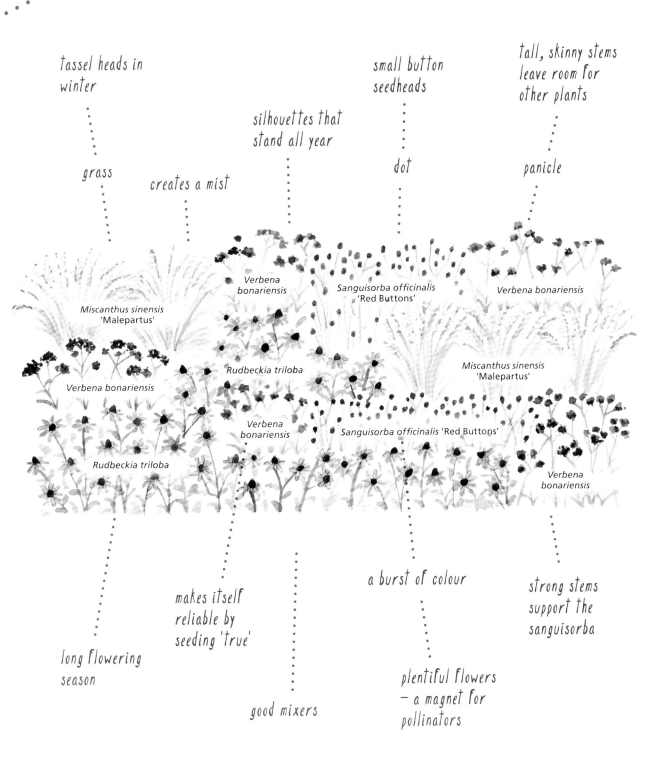

tassel heads in winter

grass

creates a mist

silhouettes that stand all year

small button seedheads

dot

tall, skinny stems leave room for other plants

panicle

Verbena bonariensis

Miscanthus sinensis 'Malepartus'

Sanguisorba officinalis 'Red Buttons'

Verbena bonariensis

Verbena bonariensis

Rudbeckia triloba

Miscanthus sinensis 'Malepartus'

Verbena bonariensis

Sanguisorba officinalis 'Red Buttons'

Rudbeckia triloba

Verbena bonariensis

makes itself reliable by seeding 'true'

a burst of colour

strong stems support the sanguisorba

long flowering season

good mixers

plentiful flowers – a magnet for pollinators

How many plants?

It's important to match each plant with a suitable space in the soil so it has room to reach its full potential but still knit together with other flowers nearby. When you first see your plants in their pots, though, it can be difficult to imagine how tall and wide they will eventually grow.

The size of a plant depends on its physiology and also its growing conditions. A plant that has plenty of space and light and the right soil will always be healthier and stronger than a plant that has been crammed in and has to compete for water and light. A plant that's happy will quickly fill the gap in the soil it has been allocated and jostle together amiably with its companions.

Even if you are not planning to plant everything in one go it's best to calculate how many plants you will need before you start. Your plants will benefit from the correct spacing and it's less tempting to plant too closely to fill the space and then have to move things about later on.

Work out the size of your garden in square metres or feet. You can refer to your plan and original measurements for this. Calculate the size of the space you've allocated to each type of plant. Because you are planting the same flowers in repeating, geometrical blocks this should be straightforward. You can round up or down a bit – you don't have to be too exact.

Referring to the number of plants per square metre/square feet given in the plant descriptions on pages 30–95, calculate the number in relation to the size of the block you've allocated for them.

For example, perovskia = 4 per m^2

MEASUREMENTS	AREA	NUMBER OF PLANTS
0.75 × 1m	$0.75m^2$	3 plants
1m × 1m	$1m^2$	4 plants
1.5m × 1m	$1.5m^2$	6 plants
1.5m × 1.5m	$2.25m^2$	9 plants

All new planting should have some empty soil between the plants, but with the correct spacing everything will knit together and you soon won't be able to see the grid you used to plan your garden.

Sourcing plants

DIY superstores, independent nurseries, garden centres and online suppliers are all useful sources of plants. Buying in person is a good option if you want to plant your garden on occasional days when you have a few hours to spare. Without a delivery charge, you can shop for a few plants at a time, as and when you are ready. A trip to a specialist perennial nursery is a lovely way to spend an afternoon; you are likely to find many of the plants you want and the staff will usually be more than happy to give you extra advice about the plants you want to grow. The plants are often displayed in really inspirational combinations that make a good source of ideas. Most nurseries will save plants for you if you phone ahead or even grow you a plant that is out of stock at no extra charge.

Choose plants with strong, heathy growth and bright green leaves, with their roots in damp compost that does not have any weeds on top. Plants that have been in their pots too long can start to turn yellow as they have used up all the nutrients in their compost. Look for plenty of new growth and shoots around the base of the plant; this is more important than lots of flowers in evidence. A few fine roots poking out from the holes in the base are nothing to worry about.

The big advantages of buying online are that the ordering process is quick and the choice is huge; plants in containers can be delivered all year round. It's disappointing to head out to local sources with an exciting list to find that some plants are not stocked or have already sold out. Most garden centres only sell plants when they are in full flower, so it can be difficult to get everything you want. Compared with a wasted trip, pulling the tape off a box delivered to your door and finding lots of healthy, bright green leaves inside feels like a real treat.

LEFT A box of mail-order *Nepeta nemorosa* 'Walker's Low' and *Eryngium agavifolium*.
RIGHT Open the box as soon as you can after the plants arrive and move them into the daylight. Carefully unwrap the packaging, taking care not to damage the delicate leaves inside. Any squashed leaves or stems will quickly straighten up.

There is normally a flat fee delivery charge, so try to group everything into as few orders as possible. Delivery times are usually 3–10 days after ordering, so you will need to plan ahead to make sure your plants are ready when you are. Open the packaging as soon as the plants arrive, even if you're not ready to start planting straightaway. They will need a little nurturing after their journey, so lift them carefully from their wrappings and give them a drink of water. Stand them outside in a cool, sheltered spot and keep their compost damp until you are ready to start planting them.

Both at nurseries and online, it's not uncommon to see a plant sold in two sizes. A plant in a 20cm/8in pot will be more fully grown than a plant in a 9cm/3½in pot, so it will be more expensive, to take account of the nursery's time and care. Fortunately, the 9cm/3½in pot size is perfect for a garden that's fully established in a year. By their very nature, perennials are plants that fill out quickly, soaring up and flourishing fast. They catch up with plants in bigger pots in no time, and they settle into the garden more quickly, too.

Give the plants a good soak. Stand them in a sheltered spot to help them recover from their trip.

Set the plants out in their pots so that you can see the overall effect before you begin.

Practical planning

The way you lay out your plants is as important as what you've chosen. It's tempting to start putting new arrivals in the soil straightaway, but it's worth taking some time at this point to get their layout and location right. It's not about puzzling over the exact spot for every plant, but creating some ups and downs, and rhythm and balance. The work you've done on your plan means you will already have a mix of shapes and groups, but there's nothing like having your plants in front of you to help you work out the best places for them.

Keeping your plants in their pots, stand them out on the soil according to your plan. Then, thinking about the garden as one whole space, consider whether you want to move any about. Points to check are:

- **Groups** Are your big groups big and bold enough? Do your smaller groups repeat and do your individual flowers pop?
- **Repeats** Have you used the same plants in several places? Have you repeated combinations more than once?
- **Echoes** Do the shapes of your flowers echo those nearby? Two different spikes planted next to each other will emphasize the spikiness of both.
- **Contrasts** Do the shapes of your flowers contrast with others? A flathead with a panicle will show off the architecture of both.
- **Height** Are there groups of shorter plants and others that are really jumping up? Have you included some variation of height? The spaces between groups of taller plants are as important as the tall groups themselves.
- **Front and back** Is there height at the front? Tall plants are good towards the back of the space but they can be even more useful at the front where other flowers can be glimpsed through them.

Step back and look your garden with a critical eye. Go inside and look at it from the windows. Check what you'll see first when you come out of the door. Make sure you're happy with everything before you dig that first hole.

How to plant

PLANTING IS A VERY SIMPLE PROCESS. ALMOST ALL
PERENNIALS CAN BE PLANTED IN THE SAME WAY: DIG
A HOLE THAT'S BIG ENOUGH, TEASE OUT SOME OF THE
ROOTS TO ENCOURAGE NEW ONES TO GROW AND PROVIDE
A THOROUGH SOAKING WITH A FULL CAN OF WATER.

All new planting will look a bit sparse
to start with, but it's important to leave
enough room between the plants to allow
them to fill out and grow (see the spacings
given in the plant descriptions on pages
30–95).

Keep watering all the plants until you
see new green leafy growth at the tips.
This usually takes one or two weeks. It's
always better to thoroughly soak the soil
around the base of the plant every few
days with quite a lot of water; sprinkling
just a small amount on the surface more
frequently just encourages shallow roots
to grow and makes plants less able to look
after themselves in the longer term. They
will take a couple of weeks to settle in, and
after that the rain will do all the hard work
for you.

Nepeta racemosa 'Walker's Low'

kit

TROWEL OR SPADE
WATERING CAN
AN ASSORTMENT
OF PLANTS

First soak the plants with water while they are still in their pots; the water should run out of the holes in the base of the pot. Leave to stand for a few minutes.

Dig a hole to the same depth as the pot and twice as wide. This will make sure that the plant will be at the same level in the soil as it was in its pot, surrounded by loosened soil that makes it easy for the roots to spread.

Free the plant from its pot. If it doesn't come out easily, giving the pot a sharp tap usually helps. Use your fingers to tease out some of the roots from the rootball. This is especially important if they have coiled around inside the pot.

Put the plant in the hole and backfill with soil. Use your hands to gently firm everything in, taking care not to push the soil down so much that you squash the air out of it or damage the plant's roots.

Soak the soil around the plant, using a full can of water. This helps to settle the soil around the rootball and encourages new roots to grow.

Planting bulbs

INSIDE EACH BULB IS A TINY SHOOT WITH A BUD WRAPPED IN STORAGE LEAVES, WAITING TO GROW WHEN THE TIME IS RIGHT.

It's important to plant your bulbs outside before winter comes, as the colder temperatures are key to starting the flowering process. I always aim to have mine in the soil by late autumn.

It's best to plant bulbs in groups of six or more, rather than dotting them individually about. Most need to be spaced 15cm/6in apart. You might put some a bit closer together or others slightly further apart to stop the flowers looking too regimented when they eventually shoot up and bloom.

Dig the hole twice as deep as the height of the bulb and gently place the bulb in the bottom, pointed end upwards as this is where the shoot and leaves will emerge. Refill the hole with soil, gently firming to make sure there are no air pockets that could fill with water and cause rotting.

Allium hollandicum 'Purple Sensation'

kit

TROWEL
BULBS

A nectaroscordum bulb

A tulip bulb

Scatter all the bulbs on the soil before you start planting. Planning where each bulb will go before you start helps you to get the spacing right.

Dig a hole twice as deep as the bulb's height. Many bulbs have contractile roots that will pull them down to the perfect depth once they're settled in the soil.

Place the bulb in the bottom of the hole and carefully replace the soil.

Hello new garden

ABOVE **Early summer**
A brilliant and wild garden flowers for longer
on stronger stems and it's happiest when you
don't water it once the plants are established:
Eryngium agavifolium, *Rudbeckia occidentalis*,
Nepeta racemosa 'Walker's Low', *Salvia nemorosa*
'Caradonna', and *Salvia* × *sylvestris* 'Viola Klose'.

RIGHT **Early summer**
Happy company: *Nectaroscordum siculum*, pom-
pom *Allium cristophii*, *Geranium* 'Brookside' and
purple salvia.

LEFT **Early summer**
A garden works best when the palette of plants is limited: *Salvia nemorosa* 'Amethyst' and *Rudbeckia occidentalis.*

RIGHT
Early summer
From around your ankles in spring to tall by summer: *Knautia macedonica* and *Phlomis russeliana.*

LEFT **Early summer**
Super-long-flowering
Geranium 'Brookside',
Salvia nemorosa
'Amethyst', *Rudbeckia
occidentalis* and *Stipa
tenuissima* provide
variety of shape and
height.

RIGHT **Early summer**
Positioned cheek by
jowl, plants help each
other out: *Echinacea
pallida*, *Verbena
bonariensis*, *Salvia
nemorosa* 'Caradonna'.

BELOW **Midsummer**
Plants with strong shapes create the structure of
the garden: *Nepeta nemorosa* 'Walker's Low', *Salvia*
'Amistad', *S. nemorosa* 'Caradonna', *S.* × *sylvestris*
'Viola Klose' and *Echinacea pallida*.

BELOW **Early Autumn**
Finding each plant a suitable space and using
successful combinations make for a garden
that is self-sustaining: *Miscanthus sinensis* and
Verbena bonariensis.

Wildlife

THE CONSTANT PARADE OF INSECT LIFE MAKES THE BRILLIANT AND WILD GARDEN AN AMAZING SPACE TO BE.

Buzzing bees, darting hoverflies and clouds of ladybirds, lacewings and butterflies visiting the flowers and stopping for lunch; it's fascinating to watch a bumblebee flying from flower to flower drinking nectar and gathering pollen, or a tiny solitary bee squeezing into the narrow corolla of a salvia searching for food to parcel up for its young.

   Plants and insects have evolved together over millions of years. The former provide food, shelter, nesting and mating sites, and in return the latter distribute pollen far and wide, enabling the plants to survive and spread. An average town or city garden has around one hundred different insect visitors, but when you make your planting areas bigger, fill them with flowers that knit together, plant like with like to make groups and leave your plants' winter skeletons intact you can expect many more. Plus, a garden that's busy with pollinators will be alive with many other creatures too. Worms will turn over your soil so you don't have to, blackbirds will keep tricky customers such as slugs and snails in check and ladybirds and lacewings will gobble up aphids. The more fluttering, flapping, chomping, chirping and buzzing you encourage in your outdoor space, the happier your flowers will be.

Eryngium agavifolium is brilliant for pollinators in summer and later in the year the strong winter seedheads make an excellent spot for a spider to spin a web.

Pollinator flowers

Choosing flowers with particular shapes and colours and planting them in patterns means welcoming the widest possible number of different creatures into your garden. Flowers are at the heart of the garden in a year, which is brilliant news for wildlife as well as for us.

SHAPES

Bold saucers, long trumpets and big colourful cups with centres of fragile stamens – it's tempting to think that flowers produce these features just for us, but in fact they are there to attract and accommodate different shapes and sizes of insect. There is enough room in the dangling bell flower of a nectaroscordum for a large, fluffy bumblebee to crawl completely inside, but only the long, thin proboscis of a butterfly can reach the nectar at the bottom of a narrow verbena floret. Hoverflies have tiny mouthparts which are a good match for the small, packed flowers of an achillea or a sedum, but it takes a stout bee buzzing furiously

The narrow corolla of *Salvia* 'Amistad'

Astrantia major 'Large White'

among the petals of a tulip to shake its stamens enough to release a shower of pollen. Helenium has landing platforms for lacewings in its petals, salvia offers spikes for hoverers, phlomis requires a heavier weight to trigger its florets to open to give access to pollen. Filling the brilliant and wild garden with different flower shapes not only makes it beautiful for us but means it will also appeal to every insect around.

NUMBERS

For wildlife, a small space that's full of flowers is a double whammy of delights. Produce a flower and a bee will always find it – you only have to look at a stall selling bunches of flowers in the middle of a city to see that this is true. But planting your garden using repeated groups of plants creates pools of colour that are easy for insects to spot. Swirls of a single type of flower tell a pollinator that this a good chance of dinner and there is likely to be plenty to eat. Flying from flower to flower uses a lot of energy, so massed flowers always make a good bet. Contrast this with a border that has bare soil and one or two plants dotted about within it – not an attractive proposition if there is something better nearby.

The bee-blue *Salvia* × *sylvestris* 'Viola Klose'

Veronicastrum virginicum 'Album'

Rudbeckia occidentalis

NECTAR AND POLLEN

Sometimes new cultivars of traditional garden flowers are of little use to wildlife. They are often sterile or have little pollen or nectar because they haven't been bred with pollinators in mind. Pollen is fed by bees to their young as a source of protein and butterflies, bees and hoverflies use sugary nectar for energy, but a sterile flower has little or none of either. With their simpler shapes and wilder characters, brilliant and wild flowers will keep foragers happy and fed. Single flowers – those with a single row of petals – are much better for visiting insects as it's less of a struggle for them to reach the middle of the flower. In most double flowers the nectaries at the base of each petal have disappeared to be replaced by more petals so there's less inside to forage.

FLOWER-PACKED

The bold shapes of umbels, spikes, dots and panicles are made up of lots of very small flowers, known as florets, held together. More often than not they open sequentially on a single plant. A veronicastrum blooms from the bottom up, while rudbeckia and echinacea open in concentric rings. Pollinators can revisit the same flower on subsequent days and have a second or third lunch.

BLOOM TIME

You can expect 20 weeks of non-stop flowers from a nepeta or a verbena, and more than 10 weeks of blooms from a knautia, origanum, veronicastrum or stachys. The bottlebrush flowers of an actaea open for 8 weeks in late summer, and a helenium has 12 weeks of

Echinops ritro

blooms. In a small garden it is even more important to have plants that bloom for a long time and the flowering periods of many perennial plants are incredibly long.

Most gardens are useful to pollinators for a month or two during the high days of summer, but with 200 days of flowers the brilliant and wild garden offers foraging opportunities even at the extremes of the seasons. A bumblebee queen searching for a nest site will choose a spot within 400 metres/¼ mile of a sustainable source of nectar and pollen for the life of her colony, which is about seven months. From the first early tulip to the last late dahlia via knautia, echinops and anemone, the medley of intermingling plants will make your garden a good choice.

WINTER BENEFITS

Plants with strong stems and architectural flowers keep their seedheads through the colder weather until new growth starts again the following spring. The hollow stem of a mathiasella or an eryngium is a warm dry haven for a beetle or hibernating solitary bee. Ladybirds nest in the seedheads of an astrantia, while the skeleton flower of a fennel is a good place for a spider to hang its web. During the coldest days when food is scarce you will spot finches, tits and sparrows feasting on the seeds left behind from summer's flowers.

Field guide

It's useful to know which creatures are visiting your garden. Identifying a lacewing as it lands on a leaf or a particular butterfly as it pauses to pump its wing on a flower can open up a whole new world. Recognizing your visitors and watching how they work in tandem with your flowers will make you love your garden even more. And when you understand their activities and see what they can do, it'll make looking after your garden even easier.

BEES

We often think of bees as living in hives and producing honey, but there are more than 250 different species of wild bee in the UK. They include more than 200 different solitary bees, 25 types of bumblebee, but just two different honeybees.

BUMBLEBEES
Bumblebees are big and furry, usually with yellow and black stripes and white tails. If you spot a bee foraging in bad weather it is most likely to be a bumblebee as their fuzzy coats keep them warm on colder days when solitary bees and honeybees don't fly. You'll often see a bumblebee that looks dusty with pollen. As they squeeze into flowers to fill the pollen baskets on their legs, the flower's anthers brush against their coats.

A bumblebee colony is made up of many smaller bees – workers and drones – and one ruling queen. In spring it's not unusual to see a queen recently emerged from hibernation clinging to the side of a flower, in need of her first sip of nectar. Smaller worker bees begin to fly in early summer, and they are on the wing until autumn.

The bumblebees you are most likely to see are the common carder, the buff-tailed and the red-tailed.

Common carder bumblebee
Bombus pascuorum
Carder bees are the most prolific bumbles in the UK. They are small black and gingery-yellow bees with stripes. Look for them buzzing around tubular flowers such as salvia, stachys and nepeta from early spring to late autumn. They have long tongues and are able to lap the nectar from deep within trumpet blooms that bees with shorter tongues struggle to reach. If you see a small, scruffy-looking bee later in summer, it's likely to be a carder as they lose patches of their fur squeezing in and out of narrower flowers.

Buff-tailed bumblebee *Bombus terrestris*
Buff-tailed bumblebee queens are out and about from late winter to mid-autumn, joined by the worker bees from early summer. The latter are just black and yellow – only the queen has a creamy-buff tail. The workers favour simple flowers with open shapes such as knautia, scabious, echinacea, helenium and single dahlias because their tongues are comparatively short. Buff-tailed bumbles will sometimes 'rob' the nectar from flowers where it is deep inside by biting a hole in the base of one of the petals, just above the stalk.

Red-tailed bumblebee *Bombus lapidarius*

Red-tailed bumblebee queens and workers are easy to identify as they are completely black with rusty red-tails. The red-tailed queen is a big bee, emerging three or four weeks later than other bumble queens, in late spring. Expect to see red-tailed bumbles until autumn on plants such as alliums, cardoons, echinops, eryngiums and other easily accessible composite flowers.

SOLITARY BEES

Most bees in the UK are solitary bees. Very fast fliers, they are on the wing in early spring, looking for a place to make a nest and then for pollen and nectar. The females use hollow plant stems to build nest cells. They leave a cake of pollen inside each cell and lay one egg in each. As soon as their larvae hatch they have something to eat. There are over 100 different types of solitary bee but the ones you are most likely to spot are the red mason bee, the leaf-cutter, the wool carder and the hairy-footed flower bee.

Red mason bee *Osmia bicornis*

Mason bees are incredible pollinators, thought to be more than 100 times more efficient than honeybees. They are ginger and furry. The females have black faces and small horns on the front of their heads. Look for red mason bees in early spring, visiting many different flowers. It is a very common bee to spot from early spring to early summer.

Leaf-cutter bee *Megachile* species

Coloured orange and black, leaf-cutter bees are quite small. They have wide black heads and big jaws with which they chew neat circles out of leaves and stems, gathering plant material that they use to build and seal up their nests. Spot them from early to late summer hunting for pollen and nectar on many different flowers.

Wool carder bee *Anthidium manicatum*

Their name was gained because these bees love soft, felty plants such as stachys, perovskia, salvia, achillea and nepeta. They pluck, or 'card', the tiny hairs from the leaves and use them to line the nests they build for their young, carrying the gathered hairs back to the nest in a ball beneath their abdomens. Carder bees collect pollen and nectar by crawling inside tubular flowers. They are big bees with yellow and black fur. You will see them from late spring to late summer.

Hairy-footed flower bee
Anthophora plumipes

This is a big bee that flies very fast, darting quickly from flower to flower. The females have black bodies and orange-red hairs on the hind legs, while the males are brown with cream markings on the face and a dark tail. As they approach flowers their long proboscis often protrudes from the mouth in anticipation of the the treats to come. They are one of the earliest bees to emerge each year and you might even see one at the end of winter. They fly until early summer.

HONEYBEES *Apies mellifera*

When we imagine a bee we typically think of a honeybee that lives in a hive and makes honey. Honeybees are quite small, with orange and black stripes. During a single collection flight they will visit 50–100 different blooms, refueling on nectar as they go. They have short tongues and so love flowers with simple, open shapes such as rudbeckias, echinaceas and anemones, but they will visit many different flowers. You will see them from mid-spring until early autumn.

LADYBIRDS
Coccinellidae species

The ladybirds you are most likely to see in your garden are the red and black seven-spot, the two-spot and the harlequin. The last has many more spots than British native ladybirds and is a troublesome pest, hugely outcompeting them and putting them at risk.

Ladybirds are one of the most useful insect visitors in the brilliant and wild garden, chomping through more than 5,000 sap-sucking aphids in a lifetime. Look for them from March to November on flower stalks, around flower buds and under the petals of freshly opened flowers – all the places where aphids gather. Although most ladybirds are red with black spots, they can also be yellow, brown or orange, or spotted with white. The larvae are mainly dark in colour but also show spots of different hues.

HOVERFLIES
Syrphidae species

As their name suggests, hoverflies can often be found hovering above flowers as if suspended in mid-air. They'll stay in one position for a few seconds before quickly darting off. They have black and yellow stripes, like a bee, but fly much faster. While they visit many different flowers to collect nectar with their long proboscis, or tongue, they favour composite flowers which have lots of tiny blooms tightly packed together. They also eat aphids in great numbers. You will see them from late spring to mid-autumn.

LACEWINGS
Chrysoperla carnoa

With skinny bodies, coppery eyes, long antennae and big, lacy wings, these insects glide around from late spring to late summer, usually towards the end of the day as dusk falls. They fold their wings back against their bodies when they land but during flight they look pearly and iridescent, reflecting the light. Spot them around buds and flowers or on newly unfurling leaves, searching for aphids to eat.

Echinacea pallida

BUTTERFLIES

Bright, still, sunny days bring butterflies out in high numbers; they rarely fly when it is windy. Butterflies feed on nectar and have a long proboscis that they unroll to reach deep within tubular flowers. They also like composite flowers such as asters, eryngiums and echinops. Although butterflies don't collect pollen, they rest their feet and legs on flowers when they sip nectar, and distribute it that way. On cloudy days you might see a butterfly resting with its wings open, trying to warm itself up ready to fly. The colourful decoration on a butterfly's wings is made up of delicate overlapping scales that reflect the light in different colours. Towards the end of a butterfly's lifecycle scales fall off, leaving transparent patches.

Painted lady *Vanessa cardui*

The painted lady is the most common butterfly in the world. It has buff-orange wings speckled with dark brown and white and arrives in high numbers in late summer. Look out for painted ladies visiting flowers such as eryngium, sedum, echinops, nepeta, verbena and aster until autumn.

Red admiral *Vanessa atlanta*

Red admirals are among the first butterflies to emerge each year. They have black wings with red bands that are speckled with white and are very fast fliers. You might see a red admiral as early as the end of spring but from midsummer onwards they are present in higher numbers, visiting densely packed flowers such as nepeta, verbena, echinops, eryngium, sedum and aster until the end of autumn.

Peacock *Inachis io*

With four brightly coloured eye-spots, a peacock is one of the easiest butterflies to identify. The markings are very striking, like the large eyes on the feathers of a peacock's tail. Their wings are dark brown beneath, so when they rest with them closed they are trickier to spot. You may see this large butterfly on any sunny day, even in winter, but most often from early to late spring then midsummer to early autumn. They like *Verbena bonariensis*, echinops, sedums and asters.

Small tortoiseshell *Aglais urticae*

These butterflies are bright orange with black spots and they fly fast. Look for them from mid-spring as they emerge from hibernation and start flying as soon as the weather warms up. They are often found in urban gardens, feeding on sedum, aster, agastache and dahlia flowers or basking in the sunshine until late autumn.

Humming-bird hawk-moth
Macroglossa stellatarum

Most moths fly at night but a few, such as the humming-bird hawk-moth, are day fliers. This is a lovely moth with a big grey and orange velvety body shaped like a bullet and pale grey wings. They beat their wings incredibly fast, so they look motionless when they hover in one spot as they dip their tongues into a flower. Because they look so large and exotic it always feels like a real treat to have a humming-bird hawk-moth visit. Look for them from early summer to mid-autumn, most particularly in late summer.

BIRDS

Most people love garden birds primarily for their song, but they're also valuable predators of garden pests.

Blackbird

Male blackbirds are black with a yellow beak and the females are brown. They are one of the biggest garden birds, present all year round. You can often see them hopping across the garden with their heads on one side looking and listening for worms or flipping leaves over to find insects beneath. They are always a welcome sight as they are brilliant at gobbling up slugs and snails, leaving the latter's empty shells behind.

Blue tit

A blue tit is a small bird with a yellow chest, pale blue wings and tail and a flash of green on its back. It's always lovely to see a blue tit because they look so bright and friendly and are useful visitors in the garden because they eat aphids. They also feed on nuts, seeds and nectar, poking their beaks inside a flower to get at the sugars – although they will sometimes nip off the whole flowerhead to achieve that. They are year-round visitors.

Sparrow

You might hear the chirp of a sparrow before you see it – or rather them, for these are intensely sociable birds. From early spring you'll see these small brown and grey birds gathering up minibeasts to take back to the nest to feed their young, while in winter they will forage in seedheads such as echinops, cirsium and miscanthus.

Robin

Finch

Goldfinches, greenfinches and chaffinches may all visit your garden. The first are the easiest to identify as have they red faces, sandy-coloured bodies and a gold stripe on each wing. They fly in a bouncy line, up and down like a wave. Finches love eating aphids in spring and summer and feast on seedheads during winter.

Robin

With its bright red breast, a robin is probably the most familiar bird of all. The fledglings in spring are plain brown. Robins are very confident and sociable and if you have one visiting your garden it will quickly make itself known. You will see them all year round.

Wren

A wren is a tiny, round bird with a long sharp beak and a tail that sticks up. They dart about quickly looking for aphids to eat. Spot them all year round.

INVISIBLE POPULATIONS

A garden that's full of bees, birds, butterflies and ladybirds will also be a magnet for myriad other creatures – invisible populations that live in the soil and help your flowers to thrive. What happens below the soil is as important as what happens above it.

Earthworms aerate your soil by pulling fallen leaves below the surface. This improves the structure, making it full of organic matter and friable (crumbly). Friable soils retain water around the roots but they don't stay waterlogged in winter or after a downpour of rain. Heavy, saturated soil makes growing hard work and too much water is more likely to kill a plant than anything else. Soil that worms have worked is a mix of minerals, organic matter, water and pockets of air that's the perfect environment for roots.

Fungi, bacteria and tiny micro-organisms recycle the leaves that the worms deliver into the nutrients that plants need. A healthy soil will have millions of micro-organisms working away at the decomposition of plant litter, creating nitrogen, phosphorus and potassium and other trace elements. These invisible workers, together with sun and rain, provide everything perennial plants need to thrive. They are an important part of your garden's ecosystem.

Earthworms are vital for healthy soil.

Working with the ecosystem

'When we try to pick out anything by itself, we find it hitched to everything else in the universe.'

JOHN MUIR, NATURALIST

While it's good to see plenty of beneficial creatures visiting your garden, others might not be so welcome. A dense cluster of aphids on a flower bud or slugs and snails devouring new green shoots and making holes in leaves can feel like a step backwards. However, if you give your plants the very best start, watering them carefully when they are newly planted and choosing plants that are happy with their neighbours, they will be much more able to shrug off trouble from pests before any serious damage is done.

It's also important to remember that every pest is someone else's lunch. All of the visitors to your garden, including those we might classify as pests, are part of its ecosystem. If there are aphids to eat, ladybirds will visit. Aphids are also a nutritious snack for young lacewings and hoverflies, and they are collected by small birds such as sparrows, robins and wrens for their nestlings. Tits eat caterpillars and song thrushes specialize in feeding on snails, cracking their shells against the ground with a sharp tap before gobbling up what's inside. Even snails and slugs are useful, though; they break down soil matter and are also a nutritious supper for beneficial ground beetles as well as birds.

If you see your plants are being eaten by predators, the best way to respond is to step back. Reaching for a chemical spray or a handful of slug pellets can seem like a good idea but in the longer term it means more work. Left to its own devices your outside space will start to keep its own checks and balances; if aphids start to increase in number more ladybirds will appear; if there is an influx of snails and slugs you can expect more blackbirds and song thrushes. Using a pesticide to pick out slugs or caterpillars or

Even visitors we might think of as pests are part of a garden's ecosystem.

greenfly or anything else upsets this balance and ultimately makes controlling pests harder work. It's much better to let the ecosystem take its course.

Chemicals sprayed on to a flower will travel around the whole plant, including into the pollen and nectar, and then leach out into the soil. The chemicals in slug pellets persist even after they have been eaten by slugs and snails and are passed on to birds. It's much better to kick off your shoes, loaf on the lawn and let everything look after itself.

Eryngium × *tripartitum*, *Nepeta racemosa* 'Walker's Low' and *Salvia nemorosa* 'Caradonna'

JOINING THE DOTS

A garden full of insect activity is fantastic news for the flowers you grow – happier, healthier blooms that always look gorgeous, and without any extra work from you. But filling your garden with flowers is good news for everyone else, too.

Grass verges, parks and those scratchy bits of earth where wildlings pop up, together with gardens like yours, create one flower-filled journey, full of pockets of green, that is vital to the important job that pollinators do. A garden full of flowers and bees is lovely if you like flowers and bees, but it's also important if you like other things such as pears, lettuces, jam or cabbages. Indeed, all of our favourite foods, and much else besides, rely on the activities of pollinators. It's essential that we help them to thrive.

Even small gardens and green spaces have a real effect on the number of pollinators that can thrive. Your own little space really is benefiting us all.

A brilliant and wild garden is great for bees, bugs and birds because:

- It's packed with flowers. More flowers means more wild visitors.
- Different shapes and sizes of flowers means plenty of different shapes and sizes of pollinators will visit.
- There is pollen and nectar even at the extremes of the seasons.
- Umbels, spikes, buttons, flatheads and composite dot flowers are made up of thousands of tiny individual florets. There are lots of chances of dinner.
- Planting in groups of 3–5 of the same plant creates large pools of colour that are easily spotted from on the wing.
- There are bee-blue flowers that are particularly visible to bees.
- The garden doesn't need pesticides and herbicides to keep it in good health.
- It's a pocket of green that acts as a pit-stop in the town or city, helping wildlife to travel far and wide.
- Strong, hollow flower stalks that stay upright throughout winter make cosy homes for hibernators.
- Long-lasting seedheads are food for hungry birds in winter weather.

Your garden is in constant flux, with something new to see each day.

Caring for your garden

A BIG PART OF THE JOY OF GARDENING IS WATCHING YOUR PLANTS CHANGE AND GROW. SEEING BULBS SHOOT, STEMS SOAR AND FLOWERS BURST INTO A MEDLEY OF COLOURS MAKES A GARDEN A WONDERFUL PLACE TO BE.

Swift to establish, the tapestry of flowers knitted together in a brilliant and wild garden will make a space that sparkles 365 days of the year. Change is everything and you can watch a whole year unfurl outside the back door.

In a traditional garden seasonal change is sometimes thought of as tricky. Gardens designed to be 'low maintenance' usually don't change much at all. They are typically planted with slow-growing evergreen shrubs that look very dull; they gradually get bigger each year and there isn't much variation to see from one week to the next. After a while we stop noticing that they are there at all. Even in a traditional garden planted with lots of colourful flowers, after spring and summer the colder, wetter weather makes everything slow down; stems are toppled by winds and rain, blooms turn soggy and collapse and plants go dormant, disappearing under the soil until spring. There's a lot of empty soil. Not many traditional gardens shine in the depths of winter.

A brilliant and wild garden, though, is a garden for every day of the year. It's like having different gardens on differerent days. Change is constant. Seeing your garden evolve day to day and week to week is a lovely way to connect with what's happening outside – a reminder that everything has a rhythm and a time, even in the middle of a town or city.

There's the thrill of bud burst, the later excitement of summer and the moment when you come back from a fortnight's holiday to find that the whole garden has soared. Then, when the weather turns colder, umbels, spikes, flatheads and panicles will hold their architectural shapes. Choosing plants such as these creates balls, spires, stars and whorls in the garden even after their flowers fade. Grown on scratchier soil, they have resilient seedheads on strong stems that are robust enough to endure the worst of the weather. Even during the coldest seasons the distinctive shapes of these flowers remain.

Less watering, less weeding, less work

In your garden doing less means having more. Bold flowers on strong stems don't need staking and shore each other up, birds and ladybirds take care of snails and aphids, and plants that are happy in their company create ecosystems where everything find its place. The flowers knit together to make a woven tapestry where there is little room for weeds. Carefully chosen plants mean they will look after themselves. It's a hands-off approach.

Although your garden will be complete within a year, it will, of course, continue to evolve beyond that point. Every spring is a chance to tidy away what's no longer useful or beautiful and to start again with a clean slate. When new green shoots start popping up at the start of the following year, it's time to give your garden a spring clean. This is a simple task that you can repeat in exactly the same way every twelve months. Cutting back winter stems and seedheads will give new growth the space it needs to flourish.

THE ANNUAL CYCLE
OF YOUR GARDEN

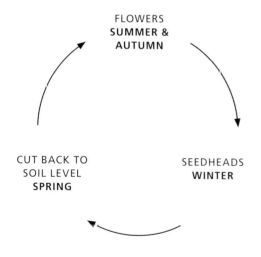

FLOWERS
**SUMMER &
AUTUMN**

CUT BACK TO
SOIL LEVEL
SPRING

SEEDHEADS
WINTER

Verbena bonariensis: cut back faded flowers in spring to give new growth space to come through.

A spring clean

When the weather and soil begin to warm up in early spring, perennial plants start preparing for the year ahead. Roots that have been dormant underground during winter produce new shoots that will grow as the days get brighter and lighter to refill your garden with flowers. Each spring, look out for small, bright green leaves around the base of your existing plants. The plants in a brilliant and wild garden get bigger every year by increasing in size from soil level. A flush of new growth appears around the crowns.

When these new shoots reach 5–10cm/2–4in high, use secateurs to cut off last year's winter stems. Cut 15cm/6in above the new flush of growth, leaving a piece of brown stalk behind. Cut chunky stems, such as those of sedums and eryngiums, individually, holding the spent flowerheads in one hand and making a clean, sharp cut with the secateurs held in the other. Twiggier stems such as origano, salvia and nepeta can be bunched into handfuls and pruned off as a clump. Cut grasses such as stipa and deschampsia into short, bristling

Sedum 'Matrona': cut off the woody stems of sedums, making a clean, sharp cut with secateurs.

Origanum 'Rosenkuppel': plants with twiggy stems, such as oregano, can be bunched together and pruned back by the handful.

Origanum 'Rosenkuppel' at the start of spring.

crops that are the same length all over. The old pieces of stalk that are left on the plants will quickly be covered by new growth and they will fall away eventually when the plant is ready. It's not important to be careful or accurate.

Because all the plants in your garden grow together, everything can be cut back on the same spring day. Gather up the cut stems and take them away.

Nepeta racemosa 'Walker's Low': you'll know it's time to cut back stems and seedheads when new shoots push up through the soil around the crowns of your existing plants.

Eryngium bourgatii: Leave 15cm/6in of the old stem on the plant rather than cutting too close to the crown. It will fall away by itself when the plant is ready.

Seedlings and wildlings

Perennial plants last for a long time, increasing in size each year. So, on the whole, they don't need to scatter seed around prolifically in order to reproduce themselves. However, some plants that are perennial but slightly shorter-lived make themselves more reliable by resowing their own patch.

The seedlings of plants such as *Verbena bonariensis*, *Dianthus carthusianorum* and *Echinacea pallida* are particularly useful as they grow into flowers that are identical to the original plants. They are described as coming 'true' from seed. Every verbena seedling will grow into a plant with the same long skinny stems and tiny violet flowers as its parent plant and every *Dianthus carthusianorum* will have the same neon pink colour-pop flowers.

Letting seeds such as this germinate and grow in the soil where they have fallen gives extra spontaneity to your garden, as they will often pop up in unexpected places.

In the early stages of the garden's development, before the plants you have chosen have knitted together, there will be some bare soil. While 'true' seedlings from the flowers you have chosen are welcome, there are likely to be some weed seedlings – wildlings – that find their way in too. It's helpful to be able to tell the weeds apart from the seedlings you want to keep.

Where are they growing?
Gravity dictates that most seeds will fall not far from the seedheads, so seedlings grouped in the soil around a particular plant are likely to be valuable. A single seedling growing on its own is more likely to have germinated from a seed that has blown in on the wind from elsewhere (like a dandelion) or arrived via a bird, stuck to its feet or feathers or present in its droppings.

What do the leaves look like?
When seeds germinate they all produce simple 'seed' leaves that nourish the plant and enable the true leaves to grow. While the seed leaves of many different plants look very similar to each other, the true leaves are always the same colour and shape as those of the parent plant. Waiting until these appear will make it easier to distinguish if the seedling is one you want to keep.

How fast do they grow?
Sad to say, a seedling that grows quickly and races away faster than the plants around it is almost always a weed!

Verbena bonariensis is a perennial but because it only lives for 2–3 years it makes itself reliable by resowing its own space.

Hints, tips & best-laid plans

The development of your garden – so exciting when it works in your favour – can seem more challenging when things don't go to plan. As you become more familiar with the plants you are growing, you'll gain the confidence to solve any problems if and when they occur. It's usually not too difficult to pin down what you need to do.

The tips of the stems and the leaves are drooping

If a plant starts to look a bit forlorn after it's been planted, this is nearly always due to lack of water around the roots. Even in quite heavy rain, the leaves on a plant can act as an umbrella and keep the soil below them dry.

Push one finger all the way into the soil next to the plant. The soil should feel cool and moist and some of it should stick to your finger when you pull it out. If the soil is dry, drench the plant using a full watering can. Water the soil directly, not the leaves and pour slowly so that the water has time to soak deeply into the ground rather than running off the surface. A thorough soaking will also encourage the plant to spread its roots outwards and downwards, seeking its own water supply from the soil in the longer term. As plants become more established and spread their roots they won't flag and droop.

A stalk has fallen over

Your plants will happily support themselves and often their neighbours too. Grown on scratchy soil, they have robust stems that act as scaffolds to keep their flowers up. But, particularly early on when your garden is finding its feet, the odd flower stem can topple over. If this happens it's usually just a case of lifting the fallen stem back up and propping it among the others.

If a stem has been lying flat for a day or two, though, particularly in summer when everything is growing super-fast, the tip will have turned a corner and started to grow at an angle from the rest of the stem. It looks a bit odd if you just stand it back up, so it's best to cut the whole stem neatly off below the bend. Use secateurs and snip about 1cm/½in above the highest leaf or pair of leaves. Side shoots will pop up from the leaf axil and later flower.

I can see the soil

All new planting schemes should have gaps between the plants at first so that there's room for everything to fill out. Perennial plants will knit together in a few short weeks. If a big gap in the soil remains you can either wait for the plants to fill it by themselves or shift a plant from another spot in the garden. The best time to move a plant that's growing is spring or autumn. Dig a hole where you want the plant to go and then dig it up from where it is now, taking a big lump of soil with its roots. Pop it in the new hole and water it in thoroughly.

Although it's tempting, avoid using plant food to boost the plants in your garden. If you keep your soil in balance and encourage plants to rely on what a healthy soil can provide, they will be better, healthier and stronger. Plants with narrow, almost leafless stems and strongly shaped flowers don't need extra fertilizer or compost – in fact, it's likely to create fast, leafy growth that's sappy, weak and more prone to aphid and slug attack, with fewer flowers and stems that struggle to remain upright.

How do I deal with pests?

Unexpected visitors are mostly welcome. They are part of the ecosystem you are creating, so don't be too quick to think they have to go. As a rule of thumb the bugs that are more useful to your flowers move more quickly, zipping about as they catch and eat pests, whereas more troublesome visitors move more slowly as they eat your plants. If you're not sure if it's friend or foe, don't squish. Aphids are unmistakable, and the best way to remove those is with a strong jet of water.

It's disappointing to see the havoc that slugs and snails can wreak on plants. Holes in the leaves or stems and shoots that have been completely devoured are sure signs that they've been at work. They are almost inevitable in the garden and it can be tempting to reach for the slug pellets. However, slug pellets contain metaldehyde and methiocarb and the disadvantage of a chemicals such as these is that even after they have done their job the toxins they contain persist. The slugs and snails that have eaten them are eaten by birds and thus they get into the food chain.

Here are a few other things you can do instead to save your flowers without causing unintended damage:

Go out after rain

Slugs and snails love wet weather, so go into your garden after a shower of rain. Look under the leaves of plants, especially lower down, and around new shoots to find them. Pick off any that you spot – wear gloves or use a folded leaf if you don't want to touch them – and drop them into a bucket of water with salt in

Holes in the leaves are a sign of slug or snail damage.

it. Some people snip them in half with scissors as a quick solution. It's your choice, depending on how squeamish you are.

Torchlight patrol

Slugs and snails come out at night, so go outside with a torch after dark and look for their silvery trails. Collect up as many as you can find, then use the salted water bucket or scissors.

Use nematodes

Nematodes are an organic method of slug control. They are microscopic worms that you buy as a powder to mix up with water

PLANTS THAT SLUGS AND
SNAILS IGNORE

Achillea	Perovskia
Actaea	Salvia
Astrantia	Stachys
Foeniculum	Thalictrum
Geranium	Veronicastrum
Nepeta	All grasses

and pour on to your soil. The nematodes predate on the slugs and will keep your garden slug-free for up to six weeks. They are a good option for the start of spring when slugs can completely devour young shoots and make it difficult for your plants to get started. Nematodes need soil temperatures of a minimum 5°C/41°F to thrive; you can order them online and they'll arrive just as the soil reaches the right temperature to use them where you live. They'll be in a sealed packet and you need to keep them in the fridge until you're ready to distribute them.

Some of my flowers are fading but other plants haven't started to flower
Gardens are a constant cycle of change and shift, and plants straddle the seasons in different ways. Flowers in full colour mixed with structural seedheads – the flux of the wild landscape – is part of what's special about your living, breathing outside space. You can stand back and let your flowers do their thing, and you will still have a brilliant garden.

However, if you want to, you can coax many perennial plants back into flower. Cutting off their faded blooms encourages them to stage a triumphant comeback and reward you with extra flowers. It is also good news for pollinators, since they visit flowers with pollen and nectar but are less interested in their seedheads. Cut off the whole spent flowerhead, snipping the stem with secateurs at the point below the flower where it intersects with a leaf or side shoot – don't just remove the very top of the flowers as this won't encourage fresh growth. If you want a bunch of fresh flowers for the house, use the same method.

From late summer onwards it's important not to cut off spent flowers so that you don't miss out on the architectural seedheads that will decorate your garden in winter.

FLOWERS THAT WILL REBLOOM
IF YOU CUT THEM BACK

Achillea	Geranium
Astrantia	Nepeta
Dahlia	Salvia

Pennisetum orientale and *Sedum* 'Matrona'

Perovskia 'Blue Spire', *Echinacea pallida, Eryngium agavifolium*

A four-season space

A brilliant and wild garden is a garden for every day of the year. It's a cycle that starts on the first day you make contact with your soil. In a small space it's even more important that a garden works as well during winter as it does in summer. There should always be something good to look at.

You can start your garden on any day of the year as long as the ground isn't frozen. Here's what to expect in the first twelve months.

SPRING

Even people without a garden anticipate spring's brighter days and increasing temperatures. Spring can offer a mixture of very cold days that still feel part of winter and warm, sunny ones when you can go outside without a coat. Plants respond to the weather and start growing when conditions are in their favour, the mix of sunshine, showers and lengthening days spurring them into growth. In early spring look for shoots appearing around the crowns of your plants, like a patchwork of green marking their spots in the soil. You'll be able to see the patterns you used to lay out your garden, which makes it easy to remove any weeds if you need to.

Below ground, as the soil temperature increases, plants start spreading their roots. The first bulbs push up, followed by the earliest perennials. Bumblebee queens start to visit, fresh from the hibernation of winter and looking for nectar for energy to fly. They'll find it in your flowers.

By the end of spring the whole garden soars. Goodbye soil!

Sedum seedheads

STARTING YOUR GARDEN IN SPRING

- New roots are encouraged to grow as the soil temperature increases.
- Smaller plants need less water to settle them in.
- Plants start growing straight away.
- The plants you want are all likely to be available; favourites won't have already sold out.
- Everything will knit together right from the start.

SUMMER

As summer progresses the garden is a kaleidoscope of shapes, with large numbers of plants in full flower, jostling for space. Umbels weave into dots, spires reach for the skies. Bees and hoverflies are out in force, followed by lacewings, ladybirds and all kinds of butterflies.

From midsummer the first of the seedheads appear as plants such as alliums enter a new phase of life. Many grasses are flowering, while others are leafing up.

AUTUMN

As the weather cools colours in the garden become more muted. Petals drop and flowers transform into seedheads.

Grown with strong stems in hungry soil, the garden stands tall. The shapes of the flowers have sharp definition: dots, stars, spikes and whorls. Hibernators seek out hollow stems

Dianthus carthusianorum, Echinops ritro, Miscanthus and *Stipa gigantea*

STARTING YOUR GARDEN IN SUMMER

- Plants are in flower when you visit the nursery or the garden centre so you can see what they look like.
- It's easy to try out combinations before you buy by standing the plants together in their pots and assessing them.
- You can quickly get a good idea of how your finished garden will look.
- Plants are bigger and less vulnerable to slugs and snails.

STARTING YOUR GARDEN IN AUTUMN

- Plants are growing less quickly and with autumn rains they need less watering to establish.
- Self-seeders such as verbena and dianthus have the chance to drop their seeds.
- You can plant bulbs now.

as cosy spots for winter. Spiders hang webs and ladybirds nestle into skeleton umbels, hunkering down before the frost.

WINTER

Grasses bleach, seedheads harden and turn black. As a stylized version of the flowers that were there before, they decorate a garden turned monotone. Frosty weather makes seedheads sparkle and show off their shapes. It's wonderful to venture outside on days when it's crunchy underfoot to see your plants glittering. A blanket of snow turns plants into hills and domes. As the weather gets cold, stems and seedheads above the soil work hard to protect what's down below. Naked crowns of plants can be vulnerable to the cold and wet.

Despite the short, dark days and freezing temperatures winter is a season of renewal. The chilly blast prepares the garden for a new cycle of growth in the spring.

STARTING YOUR GARDEN IN WINTER

- It's the best time to dig new borders.
- Frost will break down heavier soils before you start planting.
- There's no better way to spend a dark winter afternoon than sketching a plan and writing a list of the plants you want to grow.

Growing flowers on hungrier soil creates strong, resilient seedheads and stems that keep standing tall during the coldest weather.

Once planted, the perennials of the brilliant and wild garden will return bigger and better each year.

Beyond the year

A GARDEN WHERE THE PLANTS KNIT TOGETHER AS THEY GROW LARGELY LOOKS AFTER ITSELF.

Although your garden will be fully established in one year, of course it will continue to evolve. Because your plants are perennial, they'll come back year after year without your having to do anything. You won't need to replace them with new ones, protect them from frost in winter or prune them according to complicated rules to make sure they keep flowering. You won't need to give them extra food. The plants will continue to grow according to nature's rules.

The bulbs that push up in early spring will use their leaves to photosynthesize and feed themselves under the open skies. Even bulbs that flower a bit later, such as allium, produce their leaves early so they don't have to compete for resources with other plants. Shorter-lived perennials, like verbena, will gently scatter their seeds and resow their spots so you'll still keep the same medley of plants.

Most plants with fibrous roots – such as salvia and perovskia – will get bigger each year but because they only grow from around their crowns they won't take over and compete with other plants for extra space, or pop up unexpectedly in places where you'll need to pull them out. (An exception is knautia, which self-seeds madly.) Plants with tap roots, for example eryngium

and fennel, will become taller and bolder in subsequent years but they'll only grow at the tops of their roots. Think extra height and more flowers but not pushing and shoving for space. Plants with roots that grow horizontally just below the surface of the soil, such as anemones and grasses, are brilliant at filling gaps with new shoots and leaves and more flowers. Each year you can expect the plants in your garden to mingle more and flower more and just get better and better. Planted cheek by jowl, they'll also keep each other in check.

Just as in the wild, the plants in your garden will organize themselves to their advantage. Some will move towards the sun, others will resow themselves if they find a patch of soil they like. Phlomis will push for extra room; rudbeckia will grow as tall and as fast as it can to be the first to grab a pollinator's attention. A persicaria will cover the soil to stop others getting too close. Every plant works for its own benefit, but also for that of the whole community.

A garden that's full of plants that are happy in their company will manage itself without much help from you. Simply keep cutting it back on a single day every spring and it will do everything else for you, year on year.

Flower calendar

Knowing what flowers when, or how long seedheads will last, is useful when you are deciding which plants will work together.

F = flowers
S = seedheads

Echinops ritro is still in bloom when other perennials have produced their seedheads.

	mid-winter (Jan)	late winter (Feb)	early spring (Mar)
UMBELS			
Anthriscus			
Astrantia	S	S	S
Eryngium	S	S	S
Foeniculum	S	S	S
Mathiasella	S	S	S
SPIKES			
Actaea	S	S	S
Agastache	S	S	S
Nepeta			
Perovskia	S	S	S
Persicaria			
Phlomis	S	S	S
Salvia	S	S	S
Stachys	S	S	S
Veronicastrum	S	S	
DOTS			
Anemone	S	S	S
Cirsium			
Dianthus	S	S	S
Echinacea	S	S	S
Echinops	S	S	S
Geranium			
Helenium	S	S	
Knautia	S	S	S
Rudbeckia	S	S	S
FLATHEADS			
Achillea	S		
Origanum	S	S	S
Sedum	S	S	S
PANICLES			
Sanguisorba	S	S	
Thalictrum			
Verbena	S	S	S
GRASSES			
Briza			
Deschampsia	S	S	S
Miscanthus	S	S	S
Molinia	S		
Panicum	S	S	
Pennisetum			
Stipa	S		
BULBS & TUBERS			
Allium			
Dahlia			
Nectaroscordum			
Tulip			

mid-spring (Apr)	late spring (May)	early summer (Jun)	midsummer (Jul)	late summer (Aug)	early autumn (Sept)	mid-autumn (Oct)	late autumn (Nov)	early winter (Dec)
	F	F	S	S	S	S	S	S
	F	F	F	F	F	S	s	S
		F	F	F	S	S	S	S
			F	F	S	S	S	S
	F	F	F	S	S	S	S	S
					F	F	S	S
			F	F	F	F	S	S
		F	F	F	F	F	S	
			F	F	F	F	S	S
			F	F	F	F		
F	F	F	F	F	S	S	S	S
		F	F	F	F	F	S	S
		F	F	F	F	S	S	S
			F	F	F	S	S	S
					F	F	F	F	S
		F	F	F	F	S		
		F	F	F	F	S	S	S
		F	F	F	F	S	S	S
			F	S	S	S	S	
	F	F	F	F	F	F		
		F	F	F	S	S	S	S
			F	F	F	S	S	S
			F	F	F	F	S	S
		F	F	F	S	S	S	S
		F	F	F	F	S	S	S
			F	F	F	F	S	S
		F	F	F	F	S	S	S
		F	F	F				
	F	F	F	F	F	S	S	s
	F	F	F	S	S	S	S	S
		F	F	F	S	S	S	S
			F	F	S	S	S	S
			F	F	S	S	S	S
				F	F	S	S	S
			F	F	F	S	S	S
		F	F	S	S	S	S	S
	F	F	S	S	S	S	S	S
				F	F	F	F	
	F	F	S	S				
F	F							

Plant choices

PLANTS TO LOOK THROUGH
Deschampsia cespitosa 'Goldtau'
Knautia macedonica
Sanguisorba officinalis 'Red Buttons'
Stipa gigantea
Verbena bonariensis
Verbena rigida

FLOWER FOR TEN WEEKS OR MORE
Anemone hupehensis var. *japonica* 'Pamina'
Astrantia species
Echinacea pallida
Helenium 'Moerheim Beauty'
Knautia macedonica
Nepeta racemosa 'Walker's Low'
Perovskia 'Blue Spire'
Persicaria amplexicaulis 'September Spires'
Sanguisorba officinalis 'Red Buttons'

BEST COLOUR POPS
Allium hollandicum 'Purple Sensation'
Astrantia major 'Claret'
Dahlia 'Roxy'
Dianthus carthusianorum
Knautia macedonica
Rudbeckia triloba
Salvia nemorosa 'Caradonna'

BEST FOR BEES
Achillea species
Eryngium × *tripartum*
Geranium 'Brookside'
Knautia macedonica
Nepeta racemosa 'Walker's Low'
Origanum 'Rosenkuppel'
Perovskia 'Blue Spire'
Salvia nemorosa 'Caradonna'
Salvia × *sylvestris* 'Viola Klose'
Sedum 'Matrona'

TALLER GRASSES
Deschampsia cespitosa 'Goldtau'
Miscanthus sinensis
Panicum virgatum 'Shenandoah'
Stipa gigantea

SHORTER GRASSES
Briza media 'Golden Bee'
Stipa tenuissima

LATE FLOWERERS
Actaea simplex 'James Compton'
Anemone × *hybrida* 'Honorine Jobert'
Dahlia 'Roxy'
Perscaria amplexicaulis 'Orange Field'
Sedum 'Matrona'

WINTER HOMES FOR HIBERNATING INSECTS
Agastache 'Blackadder'
Astrantia species
Eryngium species
Foeniculum vulgare 'Purpureum'
Mathiasella bupleuroides 'Green Dream'

BEST ARCHITECTURAL SEEDHEADS
Agastache 'Blackadder'
Allium cristophii
Allium schubertii
Echinacea purpurea
Foeniculum vulgare 'Purpureum'
Knautia macedonica
Phlomis russeliana
Rudbeckia occidentalis
Sedum tetractinum 'Coral Reef'

Plant heights

tall (more than 1.2m/4ft)	medium (0.6–1.2m/2–4ft)		short (less than 0.6m/2ft)
Actaea	Achillea	Nepeta	Dianthus
Anemone	Agastache	Origanum	Geranium
Cirsium	Allium	Perovskia	Stachys
Eryngium	Aster	Persicaria	Tulip
Foeniculum	Astrantia	Phlomis	
Knautia	Dahlia	Pimpinella	
Sanguisorba	Echinacea	Rudbeckia	
Verbena	Echinops	Salvia	
Veronicastrum	Helenium	Sedum	
	Mathiasella	Thalictrum	
	Nectaroscordum		
GRASSES			
Miscanthus	Deschampsia		Briza
Panicum	Pennisetum		Sesleria
Stipa gigantea			Stipa tenuissima
			Molinia caerulea subsp. caerulea 'Moorhexe'

Grasses swaying among sturdier plant forms bring movement and contrast to the garden.

RESOURCES

NURSERIES

The plants in this book are all easy to source. I favour buying from smaller, independent nurseries that specialize in perennials. The plants have usually been grown by the same people who are selling them. Many of these independent nurseries are attached to new perennial gardens which are a brilliant source of inspiration when you visit. I've listed my favourites below. You can always email or phone ahead of a visit with a list of what you want and the nursery will have the plants waiting for you to pick up when you get there. Some nurseries sell online and many will deliver your plants to you for a small charge.

Traditional garden centres also sell perennial plants but often their selections are quite limited.

Avon Bulbs
Burnt House Farm, Mid Lambrook, South Petherton, Somerset TA13 5HE
Tel. 01460 242177 www.avonbulbs.co.uk
Avon Bulbs sell a wide range of allium, nectaroscordum and tulip bulbs and dahlia tubers by mail order and online. You can order them at any time of year and they will send them to you at the right time to plant. They deliver in the UK and Europe-wide.

Beth Chatto Gardens
Elmstead Market, Colchester, Essex CO7 7DB
Tel. 01206 822 007 office@bethchatto.co.uk
www.bethchatto.co.uk
Beth Chatto is my favourite source of plants. They offer a huge selection of perennial plants that are always very healthy and well grown, with well-developed root systems. The plants are grown on the nursery in Essex. You can order online and have your plants delivered anywhere in the UK or collect them yourself. You can also visit and pick out the ones you want. A delivery of plants from the Beth Chatto Nursery is a real treat, beautifully wrapped in newspaper.

Dove Cottage Nursery and Garden
Shibden Hall Road, Halifax, West Yorkshire HX3 9XA
Tel. 01422 203553 info@dovecottagenursery.co.uk
www.dovecottagenursery.co.uk
Dove Cottage Nursery is a treasure trove of delights. There's a wonderful new perennial garden alongside, full of the best flowers and grasses. Opening times can be found on the website.

Knoll Gardens
Stapehill Road, Hampreston, Wimborne BH21 7ND
Tel. 01202 873931 enquiries@knollgardens.co.uk
www.knollgardens.co.uk
Knoll Gardens specialize in grasses and perennials. The plants are all grown on the nursery by award-winning grass expert Neil Lucus. You can visit Knoll Gardens in person and pick out your plants to take home with you, pre-order and collect when you get there, or buy online for UK delivery. There are gardens to visit planted with grasses and perennials to give you extra ideas.

Scampston Walled Garden

Scampston Hall, Malton, North Yorkshire YO17 8NG
Tel. 01944 759111. info@scampston.co.uk
www.scampston.co.uk
Scampston Hall has a walled garden that contains
a perennial meadow full of exciting combinations.
Designed by Piet Oudolf, it regrows anew every year
after it's cut back to the soil each spring. The nursery
has an excellent selection of perennial plants, all
propagated from those you can see growing in the
garden. You can telephone or email ahead so your
plants will be ready for you to collect or choose them
yourself when you get there.

Sarah Raven

Sarah Raven's Kitchen and Garden, 1 Woodstock
Court, Blenheim Road, Marlborough SN8 4AN
Tel. 0345 092 0283 info@sarahraven.com
www.sarahraven.com
For the best, boldest and most brilliant tulips and
colourful dahlia flowers, Sarah Raven is hard to beat.
Her website is mouthwatering and there's lots of
choice. Order online for delivery in the UK.

GARDENS TO VISIT

Hauser and Wirth, Somerset

Hauser and Wirth, Dropping Lane, Bruton,
Somerset BA10 0NL
Tel. 01749 814 060 somerset@hauserwirth.com
www.hauserwirthsomerset.com
The 'Oudolf Field' at Hauser and Wirth in Somerset is
a perennial meadow designed by Piet Oudolf as part
of a contemporary art gallery. Planted in 2015, it's
open all year and full of the best perennial plants in
inspirational combinations. There's a small courtyard
space planted with perennials and grasses too.

Scampston Walled Garden (see Nurseries, above)

OTHER RESOURCES

Burgon & Ball

Tel. +44 (0) 114 233 8262
enquiries@burgonandball.com
www.burgonandball.com
Burgon & Ball have good-quality gardening tools,
including secateurs, spades and trowels with lovely
wooden handles. You can buy online or check their
website for local stockists.

Nemasys Nematodes

www.nematodesdirect.co.uk
Order nematodes for slug control at any time online
and they'll be sent to you as the soil gets to the right
temperature to use them wherever you live.

INDEX

Page numbers in **bold** refer to main entries; page numbers in *italics* refer to illustrations.

pollen 140
pollinator flowers 138–41
pruning 152, *152*, 153–4, 158
purple moor grass *see Molinia*

Q
Queen Anne's lace
  see Anthriscus

R
red admiral butterfly 145
red mason bee 143
red-tailed bumblebee 143
repeats, planting in 123
robins **146**, *146*, 148
Rudbeckia 53, 58, **65**, 165
  R. fulgida var. *sullivantii*
  'Goldsturm' 65, 98
  R. occidentalis 27, *42*, 65, *128*,
  130, *132*, *140*
  R. triloba 65, *65*
  bobbles and grasses planting
  plan 116–17
  height is everything planting
  plan 118–19
  and wildlife 65, 140, 143
Russian sage *see Perovskia*

S
Salvia 18, 39, **48–9**, *128–9*, 165
  S. 'Amistad' 48, 65, *101*, 110,
  134, *138*
  S. 'Nachtvlinder' 48, *49*
  S. nemorosa 48
  S. n. 'Amethyst' 48, 110, *130*,
  132
  S. n. 'Caradonna' *15*, *39*, 48,
  48, 103, *103*, *128*, *133*, *134*,
  149
  S. × *sylvestris* 48
  S. × *s.* 'Viola Klose' *19*, *38*, 48,
  107, *128*, *134*, *139*
  S. verticillata 48
  S. v. 'Purple Rain' 48–9, 76
  maintenance 153
  unexpected wild planting plan
  110–11
  and wildlife 48, 139, 142, 143

Sanguisorba 51, 73, **74**
  S. officinalis 72, *74*
  S. o. 'Red Buttons' 104, *104*
  height is everything planting
  plan 118–19
Scabious 142
sea holly *see Eryngium*
seasons 9, 13, 27, 161–3
  early autumn planting 103,
  103, 104–5, *104*
  early summer planting 102,
  102
  midsummer planting 103, *103*
  seasonal change 151
secateurs 16
Sedum 53, **70–1**, *161*
  S. 'Matrona' *67*, *70–1*, 98,
  103, *103*, *159*
  dots and spires planting plan
  114–15
  maintenance 153, *153*
  and wildlife 71, 138, 145
seedheads 149, 158
  best architectural 98, 168
  winter seedheads 96–9
seedlings 155
Sesleria 79, **87**
  S. autumnalis 87, 102, *102*,
  105, *105*
  dots and spires planting plan
  114–15
shape of plants 23–4, 25
  medley of shapes planting
  plan 112–13
Sicilian honey garlic *see*
  Nectaroscordum
slugs and snails 148, 149, 152,
  156, *157*
  dealing with 157–8
  plants that slugs and snails
  ignore 158
sneezeweed *see Helenium*
soil 18, *18*
  digging 19
  healthy soil 147, *147*
solitary bees 143
song thrushes 148

space, filling 156
spades 16
sparrows 146, 148
spikes 38–51
  dots and spires planting plan
  114–15
  flower calendar 166–7
spring 161
Stachys **50**, 140
  S. byzantinus 50
  S. officinalis 50
  S. o. 'Hummelo' *22*, 50, *50*
  and wildlife 50, 142, 143
Stipa 79
  S. gigantea *88*, **88**, 98, *162*
  S. tenuissima 41, 79, *89*, **89**,
  132
  bobbles and grasses planting
  plan 116–17
  maintenance 153–4
summer 162
  early summer planting 102,
  102
  midsummer planting 103, *103*
supporting plants 156
switch grass *see Panicum*
Symphyotrichum **55**
  S. cordifolius 'Little Carlow' 55
  S. novae-angliae 'Violetta' 55,
  55
  see also Aster
Syrphidae species 144

T
Teucrium hircanicum 22
Thalictrum 73, **75**
  T. delavayi 98
  T. d. 'Album' 75, *75*
  T. 'Hewitt's Double' 75
tools 16, *16*
tortoiseshell butterfly, small 145
trowels 16
tubers 90–5
  flower calendar 166–7
tufted hair grass *see*
  Deschampsia
tulip *see Tulipa*

ACKNOWLEDGEMENTS

Thank you to Jo Christian, publisher at Pimpernel Press, for championing *Brilliant & Wild* from the start and gentle guidance throughout. Also to Gail Lynch and Emma O'Bryen at Pimpernel.

To Jason Ingram, an incredible photographer. You are ace. To Becky Clarke for brilliant illustrations and beautiful pages. Thank you both.

To Alice Workman, Hauser & Wirth Somerset, with kind permission from Piet Oudolf, for letting me into the Oudolf Field before and after hours.

To Lady Legard and Paul Smith, head gardener, Scampston Walled Garden, Malton – for letting me visit the garden in the depths of winter and the height of summer.

To Kim and Stephen Rogers, Dove Cottage Garden & Nursery, Halifax. The nursery is amazing, the garden beautiful. Thank you.

To Katherine Hewitt, Ian Armstrong, Julie Coulten, Louise Young, Peter Young, June Smith-Sheppard and Fiona Cumberpatch, all generous, kind and helpful in equal measure.

And, most of all, to my mum, Anne, to Bill and to big sister Victoria – I could not have written this book without you.

Echinacea pallida seedhead with
Stipa tenuissima